GEMINI
2001

With love to all my family and friends

Well, here we are for another year. Thanks to everyone who helped me with these books for the fourth year in the series. Many thanks to Nova Jayne Heath, Nicola Chalton, Nick Robinson and everyone else at Constable & Robinson – it's a pleasure to work with you. Mega thanks to Annie Lionnet and Jamie Macphail for all their input and work. Thanks to Chelsey Fox for all her agenting skills. And thanks to Bill Martin for checking all the dates.

GEMINI
2001

Jane Struthers

p

This is a Parragon Book
First published in 2000

Parragon
Queen Street House
4 Queen Street
Bath BA1 1HE
UK

Produced by Magpie Books, an imprint of
Constable & Robinson Ltd, London

ISBN 0-75254-304-0

A copy of the British Library Cataloguing-in-Publication Data
is available from the British Library

Printed and bound in the EC

CONTENTS

Dates for 2000

Gemini 20 May – 20 June

Cancer 21 June – 21 July

Leo 22 July – 22 August

Virgo 23 August – 21 September

Libra 22 September – 22 October

Scorpio 23 October – 21 November

Sagittarius 22 November – 20 December

Capricorn 21 December – 19 January

Aquarius 20 January – 17 February

Pisces 18 February – 19 March

Aries 20 March – 19 April

Taurus 20 April – 19 May

INTRODUCTION

Dear Gemini

Welcome to my astrological guide to 2001! I hope you have a fantastic year, filled with all the things you wish for.

If you have bought these books before you will see that the running order has changed this year. **Gemini 2001** begins with your day by day guide to the year, with charts at the start of each month so you can assess at a glance your prospects for love, money, career and health.

The second half of the book is packed with astrological information. In **Your Gemini Sun Sign** I explain what your Sun sign says about you, with categories describing your basic character, the way you react in relationships, your attitude to money, the state of your health and the types of career that suit you. The next chapter, **The Moon and your Relationships**, contains special charts so you can plot the Moon's path through your horoscope each month and see which relationships to concentrate on at any one time. **Love and the Stars** also talks about your relationships, describing how the Sun signs get on with each other. At the end of this chapter there are two compatibility charts showing how the signs relate to one another as lovers and friends. The final chapter is **Your Home and Family**, and in it you can read what your Sun sign says about your home and your relationship with your nearest and dearest.

With all this information, you should be all set for a marvellous 2001!

Gemini Jane

THE YEAR 2001

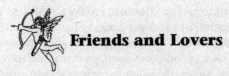 **Friends and Lovers**

Get set for a roller-coaster year in which life will be really busy and highly enjoyable. There is plenty going on in 2001, especially in the first seven months of the year when your social life reaches a peak, and the momentum from that will carry you on a high through to the end of December.

If you want a new relationship this year, the power of your personality could attract lots of people to you. The more vivacious, outgoing and gregarious you are, the more everyone will flock around you. Even if you don't meet a new love, you can be sure of making some new friends.

All Geminis are experiencing a backdrop of relationship difficulties at the moment. For instance, you may be meeting more than your fair share of control freaks who want to run your life. A partnership may be going through a sticky patch, perhaps making you realize that it's make or break time. This is especially likely if your birthday falls between 3 and 6 June. Although these experiences will be very disruptive and upsetting, try to learn from them because they will help you to sort out your priorities in life and also to discover an inner strength that you didn't know you had.

Health

You are feeling full of beans this year, and especially between January and July! You have more energy than usual and you will adore making the most of it. It's a super time for doing things that require an effort and involve a challenge. Putting yourself to the test and doing things for the first time will boost your confidence and make you feel really good about yourself.

Keep a close eye on your weight, particularly in the first half of the year. You might put on more weight than usual or you could be tempted by lots of fattening foods. Keeping active will help to burn off all those extra calories.

From late April onwards you need to take extra care of your health. Even though you will still be feeling bouncy and exuberant, there may be phases when your energy levels dip and you need more rest than usual. It might be a good idea to increase your intake of vitamins and minerals whenever this happens, but always seek medical advice if you think it's necessary.

Between July and the end of the year, try not to let any worries get you down or prey on your mind. You may feel more responsible than usual, even when it isn't necessary, which could make you feel that you have to look after other people or run around after them.

Money

This is one of those delightful years when almost everything seems to go according to plan. And finances will undoubtedly also play their part in all this. In the first half of the year you will do well if you can capitalize on the great opportunities that are coming your way. Some of them could bring money with them or they might introduce you to someone who helps you to make your fortune. If you have never thought of taking part in competitions or a lottery, this is a good time to start. You could have some wonderful strokes of luck!

Money really starts rolling in from July onwards. You might receive a huge windfall or there could be more modest trickles of cash coming your way. Unfortunately, you may not have the money for long because you will really enjoy spending it! So you might receive it with one hand and spend it with the other! If you have the money to spare, this is an excellent year for making prudent investments that will grow in value.

Be prepared to sort out your finances and tidy up any muddles in early January, early July and late December. If you want to start a new financial strategy, the end of June is the perfect time to begin.

 **Career**

So much is going on in your life this year that you may not always have much time for your career. After all, you've got to fit it in around your busy social life! Even so, if you want to impress other people with your personality, abilities and talent, this is definitely not the year for modesty. You are blessed with extra confidence in 2001 so put it to good use.

If you fancy embarking on a new career, this is a marvellous chance to begin. You are feeling adventurous and prepared to give it a shot. What's more, you don't want to waste your time on anything that is becoming increasingly tedious or which no longer holds any charms for you.

Anything connected with travel, education, religion, spirituality or politics should go well for you professionally. You might even get the urge to go back to college and study for a degree in a subject that fascinates you. There could also be a global connection with your career in 2001.

Watch out for a slight tendency to overwork, especially from April onwards. You may have an overdeveloped sense of duty at times, making you work round the clock or be the first to step into the breach when things go wrong. You want to prove that you are responsible but there is no need to work yourself into the ground!

Your Day by Day Guide

JANUARY AT A GLANCE

Love	♥ ♥ ♥
Money	£ $ £ $ £
Career	💻 💻 💻
Health	☼ ☼ ☼

• *Monday 1 January* •

Happy New Year! If you've already thought about what you'd like to achieve in the coming year but haven't come up with a concrete plan, spend the next few days devising some specific ways in which you can realize your goals. You'll have many wonderful opportunities to make some of your hopes and dreams come true in 2001. All you need is faith in your abilities and belief in yourself.

• *Tuesday 2 January* •

Keep channelling all your efforts into your hopes and dreams for the future because the more you focus on them and the more positive you are about them, the better their chance of coming to fruition. Above all, don't allow your rational mind to limit your possibilities or discount various options because they seem beyond your reach. Use your intuition to discover what's truly possible.

• *Wednesday 3 January* •

If a certain situation has been bothering you recently, you'll come up with a spontaneous solution or insight into the problem today that will ease things considerably. This will be especially helpful if you've had to work with someone who makes you feel tense or uneasy, or if there's been a nagging sense of discontent in a close relationship.

• *Thursday 4 January* •

It's a day for taking things easy and going at a gentle pace if you can. If you're busy at work you'll have a very short attention span and your mind could keep drifting off into daydreams and flights of fancy. Ideally, you'd love nothing more than to spend the day enjoying a favourite hobby or pastime, especially if it's creative or artistic. Listening to some uplifting music will be wonderfully therapeutic.

• *Friday 5 January* •

You might find it hard to ask for what you want today, hoping that others will pick up intuitively what you're not saying out loud. That's all well and good if you happen to be surrounded by psychics, but probably most people won't have a clue how to read your mind. If you want to avoid disappointment on your part, and frustration on everyone else's, do your best to speak up!

• *Saturday 6 January* •

If one of your New Year resolutions is to cut down on certain foods or alcohol and get into better shape, you might find it hard to keep your resolve today. Temptation will be everywhere you look, and if you're invited out for a delicious meal you won't have the heart to deprive yourself. Besides, you don't want to offend anyone by showing a lack of interest!

• *Sunday 7 January* •

A family member may be rather distant today and they'll stubbornly resist all your attempts to get them to open up. Or are you the one who is playing your cards close to your chest and not giving anything away? Either way, communication won't be easy and it may be wise for all concerned to let sleeping dogs lie and not try to force any issues – at least for the time being.

• *Monday 8 January* •

You're in a very positive mood today and this will be a great help if you are facing a challenging day or you want to win someone over to your side. You'll soon be bored with mundane or routine tasks, so find something to do that really stretches you mentally and gets you thinking along completely new lines. You could experience a surprising and sudden attraction to someone who isn't your type but is irresistible at the moment.

• *Tuesday 9 January* •

Focus on your finances today, particularly if you've got some outstanding bills to pay or you need to have a chat with your bank manager. It's an excellent day to think about your long-term security and ways to invest or save for the future. If you've been burying your head in the sand over a money issue, today's Full Moon could force you to get to grips with the problem once and for all.

• *Wednesday 10 January* •

You're feeling very sensitive and emotional today but you may go to great lengths to present a very different image. Perhaps you want to appear cool, calm and collected because you don't know how a certain someone will respond to you if you let your guard down. Be circumspect by all means if you feel you need to protect yourself, but try not to deny your feelings to yourself.

• *Thursday 11 January* •

Your morale gets a massive boost today, renewing your confidence and giving you something to smile about. You might enjoy a harmless flirtation with someone or be complimented on your abilities or expertise in some area. It's also a great day to make plans for a holiday abroad or a short break away. You're in the mood for adventure and going somewhere off the beaten track. Sounds like fun!

• *Friday 12 January* •

Your energy levels shoot up today and you'll feel able to tackle whatever life throws at you – no matter how challenging. If you intend to make some changes to your daily routine and you encounter some resistance from a partner or colleague, you'll have no trouble finding a watertight argument to convince them that you know best. You won't take no for an answer either if someone is trying to wriggle out of something. Talk about a tough customer!

• *Saturday 13 January* •

This is an excellent day to start any home improvement projects you have planned. Whether you're decorating or doing repairs, you're ready to make some changes and create a new look. You have lots of stamina at your disposal, so you'll be able to work extra hard and get plenty done. Be prepared to throw out anything that no longer serves a purpose.

• *Sunday 14 January* •

You're in a hard-working mood again today and you want to continue from where you left off yesterday. You can also count on the help and support of a loved one, especially if you're working as a team and have to pull together. Something they say or do will be worth its weight in gold and make you realize how reliable and trustworthy they are.

• *Monday 15 January* •

You're in a very down-to-earth mood today and you have a practical and realistic approach to what you want to achieve in the months ahead. You have both the commitment and the tenacity to get your plans off the ground, as well as the determination to make your mark. If there's anything that you're unhappy about and need to resolve, this is a good day to do something about it.

• *Tuesday 16 January* •

If you think you can keep your emotions under control today, you should think again! You're in a very sexy and passionate mood, and a close relationship will become even more intimate if you succumb to your desire to bare your soul and show how you feel. If you're currently a solo Gemini, you could be swept off your feet by someone who provokes an instant and compelling attraction in you. Heady stuff!

• *Wednesday 17 January* •

You're in a very loving and altruistic mood today, and are strongly aware of a loved one's needs. You're able to give of yourself unconditionally, especially if someone needs to talk about a very sensitive issue or wants a shoulder to cry on. You may not aware of it but others will feel better simply by being in your presence now.

• *Thursday 18 January* •

Mind how you go today because things won't run as smoothly as you would like. It's very difficult to understand what a certain person is up to because they may say one thing and do another. Or they could promise more than they can deliver, making you feel angry and let down. Let them know how disappointed you are but resist the temptation of making them feel as if they've committed a cardinal sin.

• *Friday 19 January* •

You have abundant mental energy today and you'll enjoy any kind of stimulating conversation or debate. You could even get quite het up if you're discussing anything of a philosophical or religious nature as you'll feel very passionate about what you believe in. Be careful not to sound too self-righteous though, especially if you want to win someone over to your way of thinking.

• *Saturday 20 January* •

Be careful about who you place your trust in today because you're in a rather gullible mood and someone could easily manipulate you or lead you up the garden path. It's certainly not a good day for committing yourself to anything because what you see is definitely not what you get, no matter how fascinating and inviting it might seem. Forewarned is forearmed.

• *Sunday 21 January* •

Put enjoyment high on your list of priorities today because there'll be plenty of opportunities for fun and laughter. You're in a wonderfully jovial and outgoing mood and you'll want to be in the company of like-minded people, doing things that you find stimulating and uplifting. If you meet anyone new, you'll find that you have a surprising amount in common and can bring out the best in each other.

• *Monday 22 January* •

You want to be completely your own person today. You will be at your best if you have a free rein and no external restraints to hold you in check or cramp your style. Any work that demands an innovative approach or lateral thinking is favoured and you'll pick up new information at lightning speed. This bodes well if you need to familiarize yourself with some new technology or dazzle someone with your know-how.

• *Tuesday 23 January* •

Got your wires crossed? You could be talking at cross-purposes with someone today, resulting in both of you going round and round in circles. The most likely reason for this is that one of you is adopting a purely rational point of view while the other is taking a much more intuitive approach. Rather than staying firmly in opposite camps, why not combine both perspectives? It could be an enlightening experience.

• *Wednesday 24 January* •

Today's New Moon is encouraging you to break new ground and expand your horizons. You're ready to experiment with different ideas and you'll want to get together with people who are unconventional and who can introduce you to exciting and new ways of thinking. If you're a typical Gemini, there's no doubt that this will be music to your ears.

• *Thursday 25 January* •

If someone has been testing your patience recently and you've been restraining yourself from giving them a piece of your mind, you could have no choice today but to tell them a few home truths. You may well decide that unless you take them to one side and point out to them what they're doing, they'll happily carry on in the same way *ad infinitum*. Not a prospect you savour.

• *Friday 26 January* •

It's a marvellous day for following up on your resolutions for this year and continuing to make positive changes. If you've yet to tick anything off your wish list, make a promise to yourself today to do something that will bring you one step closer to what you most want. A loved one or close friend is in a wonderfully easy-going and happy mood and you take great delight from being in their company.

• Saturday 27 January •

If you're a classic Gemini, you have an enquiring mind and an insatiable desire for knowledge. You could get a valuable insight today into what makes you tick, giving you plenty of food for thought. You might have a conversation with someone who's known you for a long time and who is able to shed light on an episode from your past. This will spur you on to find out more.

• Sunday 28 January •

Allow yourself to be guided by your intuition today and leave logic on the back burner. Much to your surprise, you could begin to feel a strong emotional connection with someone you've known as a friend or acquaintance. Although your natural response to this is to analyze why you feel this way, why not trust your feelings and see what follows?

• Monday 29 January •

You want to invest a lot of physical and emotional energy in a close partnership today, especially if it's very new or you haven't had a lot of time for each other recently. You're very aware of your emotional needs and you'll do whatever you can to make the relationship more solid and permanent. You'll also be able to reassure someone who's feeling insecure about themselves by giving them some positive feedback.

• Tuesday 30 January •

Good news! You're at your most attractive and magnetic today, and this winning formula will guarantee you a really great time. Other people will respond positively to your high degree of self-assurance and charm, and this will work in your favour both at work and in your personal life. You'll also feel strongly motivated to accomplish something you've set your heart on, and which you know is now within reach.

• *Wednesday 31 January* •

It's another day for being sociable and gregarious, and you'll want to spend as much time as you can with some of your favourite people. You won't have to do anything special together; you'll simply appreciate their company. It's also a good day for initiating anything new that will add greater fulfilment and happiness in your life. If your mind draws a blank on what that might be, your heart will come up with the answer.

FEBRUARY AT A GLANCE

Love	❤ ❤ ❤ ❤
Money	£
Career	💻 💻 💻 💻 💻
Health	☼ ☼

• *Thursday 1 February* •

It's a great day for making progress at work, especially if you're willing to say what you really think. Standing up for yourself and having the courage of your convictions will earn you both the admiration and the respect of a boss or authority figure. From now on, you'll be able to count on their support. If you realize what your next step should be, now is the time to take it.

• *Friday 2 February* •

Take care on the emotional front today because it looks as if a certain person is on the warpath. Or are you the one who is looking daggers at a partner or loved one? It's important to get any resentment or hostility out in the open because you won't want this tense atmosphere to continue for long. If you're working from home today, expect a few hiccups in your routine.

• *Saturday 3 February* •

What do have you planned for the weekend? If you're involved in any group activities, you'll find it easy to get on with everyone and you'll enjoy the convivial atmosphere. If you're doing something for the first time, you could strike up a friendship with someone who impresses you. In fact, you'll probably set up a mutual admiration society because they'll be pretty taken with you, too!

• *Sunday 4 February* •

You're in a reflective mood today and you're asking yourself some searching questions. You might become aware of a secret fear you've been harbouring and which is inhibiting or hampering your progress in some way. Discovering where this fear originates will help you to resolve the issue and remove any obstacles that are standing between you and the fulfilment of your potential.

• *Monday 5 February* •

Make the most of the dynamic energy that starts to surge through you today and you'll be able to achieve a tremendous amount. If you feel that your job doesn't bring you into contact with interesting people or offer you enough mental stimulus, it's time to start thinking about what changes you could make. You're no longer prepared to settle for less than the best.

• *Tuesday 6 February* •

Any decisions that you made yesterday will have a considerable impact on the days ahead. You may have decided that it's time to introduce some long-term changes to any area of your life that you're no longer happy with, in which case you'll want to discuss how you feel with those that are close to you. Don't be surprised if a certain someone feels threatened by your suggestions and puts up some resistance. Give them time.

• *Wednesday 7 February* •

You're in a very buoyant and lively mood today and you'll be bored stiff if you have to do anything predictable or run-of-the-mill. You're in the mood to do something completely different from your usual routine, particularly if it means getting out and about or visiting somewhere new. If you have to stay put and get on with work, try to make what you're doing as much fun as possible.

• *Thursday 8 February* •

Your moods swing backwards and forwards today as you try to unravel something that's preoccupying you. The Full Moon is highlighting your need to put your feelings under the microscope and find out why you seem to be blowing hot and cold with a certain someone. You may not come up with an immediate answer but at least you'll be taking responsibility for your rather unpredictable behaviour.

• *Friday 9 February* •

You're in the mood to let off some steam after yesterday's intense atmosphere, so do something stimulating and energetic. You'll benefit from any activities that improve your communications or connect you with people who inspire you in some way. Talking and sharing ideas are two of the things that Geminis do best, so do what comes naturally!

• *Saturday 10 February* •

It's a great day for keeping busy at home and getting all the things that need to be done out of the way. You're in a very industrious and hard-working mood, and you'll throw yourself into tasks with a vengeance. If no one is around to lend you a hand, you'll be quite happy to get on with things in your own way and at your own pace. In fact, you might even prefer it!

• *Sunday 11 February* •

Getting together with close family and friends will be great fun today, especially if you can enjoy a day out together. You'll love having a change of scene, and even spending a few hours somewhere different will recharge your batteries and make you feel as if you've had a rest. A friendship could deepen as a result of a fascinating and revealing conversation.

• *Monday 12 February* •

You're very goal-orientated today and you'll be putting your heart and soul into attaining a personal aspiration that is very important to you. Somehow you feel that now is the right time to test your ability to make a dream come true and, if you do manage to succeed in your quest, it'll give you the confidence to pursue other aims you have for the future. Good luck!

• *Tuesday 13 February* •

Stop for a moment! It is time to focus on your general well-being and what you could do to improve your current state of health. Are you working too hard or not getting enough sleep? Or perhaps you're neglecting your body and not eating enough of the things that are good for you. If you want more energy and vitality, start making some positive changes and you'll soon have a new lease of life.

• *Wednesday 14 February* •

Happy Valentine's Day! Don't be too disappointed if the postman doesn't bring you any cards because someone is about to show their commitment to you in a completely different way. You might be surprised to hear that a certain someone is a lot more serious about your relationship than they've let on before. The question is: what will you make of their unexpected announcement?

• *Thursday 15 February* •

Any plans connected with the future will move one step closer to fruition today. It's an ideal chance to take part in discussions or negotiations, because you'll easily be able to get others to agree to your terms and conditions. You'll also be glad to know that a partner or associate will come up trumps and give you their full support.

• *Friday 16 February* •

Watch what you say today because you may not be very thoughtful and you could annoy someone by saying the wrong thing. Mind you, it will probably be impossible to spend the whole time tiptoeing around and you may have to reconcile yourself to causing a slight stir. Provided you didn't intend to hurt anyone, everything will sort itself out.

• *Saturday 17 February* •

Talk about fireworks! Your libido goes through the roof today, and if you're looking for romance something exciting may be about to happen. You're in a very self-assured and confident mood so the chances are that you'll be the one to make the first move, and from then on anything could happen. Don't be surprised if the person you're irresistibly attracted to comes from a very different background or culture to your own.

• *Sunday 18 February* •

It's a day for enjoying yourself and doing things that are out of the ordinary. Life feels very exciting and full of unexplored possibilities, so you want to do something new and challenging that puts you in touch with a different aspect of your personality. If you've felt bored with the status quo recently and haven't known how to bring some zest into your life, you'll now come up with some interesting ideas.

• *Monday 19 February* •

You're in two minds about something today, making you rather hesitant to reach a decision. A certain someone can't understand why you're being so non-committal and they may try to coerce you into doing something out of sheer frustration. There's no point in going along with a plan unless your heart is really in it, so try to play for time until you have a clearer picture.

• *Tuesday 20 February* •

You're in a playful and frivolous mood today and you'll jump at the chance to get together with some friends and have some fun. You're also feeling rather extravagant and might be tempted to go on a shopping spree and buy something that will add an exciting new dimension to your life. If you're feeling flush, you'll really enjoy treating someone to a meal or a gift of some kind.

• *Wednesday 21 February* •

Make sure you tell the truth, the whole truth and nothing but the truth today because you could be caught out if you don't. You might be tempted to put a gloss on something to avoid hurting someone's feelings, but this could backfire on you if they realize that you're covering up. It's better to face the music and come clean, whatever the consequences.

• *Thursday 22 February* •

You're in the mood to take things easy and relax today, but don't let the day slip through your fingers or you could miss a golden opportunity to make an important contact. The New Moon is offering you a chance to rethink the direction you're heading in, and someone you meet by chance could be instrumental in helping you see other possibilities. Keep your ears and eyes open!

• *Friday 23 February* •

You can communicate in a very powerful and persuasive way today, and you'll be able to get your message across to even the most unreceptive ears. This bodes well if you're trying to sell yourself, promote an idea or make a presentation of some kind. You could also have some kind of breakthrough in a relationship or partnership that has been going through a sticky patch.

• *Saturday 24 February* •

It's a good day to look at your finances and make sure they're in good order. If you're feeling more in control of money matters than you have recently, why not think about how to make your money work for you in bigger and better ways? Perhaps there's an investment scheme that would yield top benefits and create a substantial nest egg for your future. Discuss your various options with someone in the know.

• *Sunday 25 February* •

It's all systems go today and, if you're a typical Gemini, you'll be able to do several things at once and get a real buzz from them. You could also come up with some fantastic ideas on how to streamline your everyday routine and make your life run more smoothly and efficiently. And if your computer hasn't been performing properly recently, you could suddenly get a brainwave about where the problem lies. Brilliant!

• *Monday 26 February* •

You are on top form today! If you're working as part of a team you'll feel on the same wavelength as everyone else. You'll be able to bounce ideas off each other in a very creative and constructive way, and you could come up with some innovative solutions to old problems. You're also feeling very sociable, so try to get out and enjoy yourself with a colleague or good friend.

• *Tuesday 27 February* •

You can benefit from someone else's experience today, especially if they're older and wiser than you and can offer you a balanced perspective on a very personal issue. Trying to come up with a solution on your own could make it harder, as you may have a blind spot about it and not recognize the root of the problem. Don't be afraid to bare your soul because what you discover about yourself could be worth its weight in gold.

• *Wednesday 28 February* •

Who's got their head in the clouds? Try not to let your imagination run away with you today or you could land with a bump when reality catches up with you. You might put someone on a pedestal and have all kinds of romantic notions about them, which are purely based on fantasy. Or you might idealize a situation, thinking that it will promise more than it could ever deliver. Take a reality check before you do anything rash.

MARCH AT A GLANCE

Love	❤ ❤ ❤
Money	£ $
Career	💻 💻 💻 💻 💻
Health	☼ ☼

• *Thursday 1 March* •

You're in a very organized and businesslike mood today, and if you have a lot of hard work to do you'll be able to apply yourself in a very focused and methodical way. This means you'll be able to plan what you're going to do in advance to avoid getting distracted and wasting a lot of time or energy. You'll also gain a lot of satisfaction from sorting out any outstanding money matters.

• *Friday 2 March* •

Try to do as much socializing as you can today because you're in a wonderfully outgoing mood. You might feel like doing some entertaining and having a group of friends round for a meal. You'll also want to make the most of your brainpower, but more in the form of play than hard work. A good general knowledge quiz or board game might do the trick.

• *Saturday 3 March* •

It's a great day for negotiations or discussions because you can express yourself in a very clear and concise way. Not only that, you're feeling very fair-minded and willing to meet people half-way on important issues, without compromising yourself in any way. You'll also experience a wonderful sense of harmony in a close relationship, thanks to your ability to listen and empathize.

• Sunday 4 March •

You enjoy a meeting of minds with someone today and you'll quite happily spend a few hours discussing your different ideas and putting the world to rights. You might also want to channel your energies into a cause or project that you believe in wholeheartedly and which totally inspires you. You want to do something that makes a difference and has a positive impact.

• Monday 5 March •

Be prepared for a few difficulties where a colleague or boss is concerned. Don't assume that you've reached a deadlock, because if you work together to find a solution your relationship will gain a much more solid footing and you'll be able to resolve your differences. You're also feeling quite thrifty now so it's a good day to hunt around for a bargain or put some money aside for a rainy day.

• Tuesday 6 March •

If you're feeling under par today, do something that will recharge your physical, mental and emotional batteries. Decide what would most energize you. If you're in need of some company, choose someone who can make you laugh and who brings out the best in you. Alternatively, you might get as much pleasure from having some time to yourself.

• Wednesday 7 March •

You want to keep on the move as much as possible today, otherwise you'll feel as if you've got stuck in a rut. Try to get a change of scenery if you can, even if it means going for a walk or taking a different route home. Perhaps it's time to think about ways to change your daily routine and incorporate more variety into it. And if you feel like seeing some new faces, why not join a club of some kind?

• Thursday 8 March •

If you have any nagging fears or worries that you haven't been able to put your finger on, they could come to the surface today and make you feel you have no choice but to deal with them. It might be a good time to have a medical check-up just to put your mind at rest, or to get things off your chest by talking to a good friend who can offer you some sound advice.

• Friday 9 March •

Relationships come under the spotlight for the next four weeks and you could be faced with some unexpected developments. A woman who you thought was a friend may turn out to have a hidden agenda, and you might realize that she's competing with you in some way. You won't necessarily be able to prove anything straightaway, so bide your time and get the measure of her before you make your move.

• Saturday 10 March •

Even if you don't have a lot planned for today, the last thing you'll want to do is relax and put your feet up because you're in the mood to do something useful instead. If there are any jobs that need doing around the house, you'll tackle them in a very industrious and systematic way. In fact, you'll be so efficient that it will probably only take you half the normal time to get everything done. And then what will you do?

• *Sunday 11 March* •

You won't want to put a lot of emotional investment into anything or anyone that doesn't seem worthwhile today. You're much more concerned with channelling your emotional energies into people that you really value and activities that you find rewarding and fulfilling. Not everyone will be happy with such an uncompromising attitude.

• *Monday 12 March* •

A wave of nostalgia sweeps over you today as your thoughts turn to the past and some very sentimental memories. You might look through some old letters or photo albums, or you may decide to get in touch with someone you haven't seen in ages. You could also be drawn to visiting a place that holds a special meaning for you and evokes an important time in your life.

• *Tuesday 13 March* •

You can make a big impression on the world today, especially if you're launching a new project or discussing your ideas with someone. You're thinking big and putting a lot of energy into realizing a goal or dream that is very close to your heart. You're also in a very assertive mood and you'll be willing to knock on doors that have remained closed until now without a moment's hesitation. That's the spirit!

• *Wednesday 14 March* •

Yesterday's enterprising spirit continues full force today and you may decide to make some sweeping changes to the pattern of your working life. Everything you do is likely to turn out well because you have the conviction that it will be a success. And the good news is that you won't have to force any issues or throw your weight around to make things happen. All you need is to believe in yourself.

• *Thursday 15 March* •

You're full of beans today and you'll want to put your energy to good use by doing something physical, such as having a good workout or doing some gardening. You'll also get bored very easily so try to avoid anything that smacks of routine or simply doesn't capture your imagination. If you're still in the throes of arranging a holiday, this is an excellent time to firm up your plans.

• *Friday 16 March* •

You could antagonize someone today simply by sticking to your principles and not being willing to compromise. Whatever the issue is, you'll refuse to budge from your position. If a loved one accuses you of acting out of character or being too rigid, try to make them understand that as far as you're concerned it would be morally wrong to do anything else.

• *Saturday 17 March* •

Someone makes a powerful impression on you today. Even if you've only just met you'll feel a strong emotional connection with them. And don't think that you'll only be exchanging social chit-chat because, before you know it, you'll be having a serious talk about subjects that are important to you both. If you're not romantically involved at the moment, this promises to be the start of something very special.

• *Sunday 18 March* •

Today marks the beginning of a new phase in your life that promises to broaden your horizons and open up your world. Look out for a marvellous opportunity that offers you the chance to fulfil a long cherished dream and bring to fruition your innate talents and abilities. The next couple of weeks could also bring a kindred spirit into your life that connects you to a part of yourself that has been dormant. Magical stuff!

• Monday 19 March •

It's another day to count your blessings and appreciate the calibre of people who are in your life at the moment. You'll want to show a close loved one how much they mean to you by giving them a gift or taking them out somewhere special. If there's been a rift between you and a certain someone and neither of you has wanted to back down, you could decide to make the first move towards reconciliation.

• Tuesday 20 March •

If you're a typical Gemini you easily get bored, but there's no chance of that today because you could hear some news that sends you into a flurry of activity. You might receive a letter saying that you've been accepted for a new job or that you're about to exchange contracts if you're in the middle of a move. You could also receive an invitation to visit a country you've never been to before. How exciting!

• Wednesday 21 March •

There is a change in the air and you feel excited by all the new developments that are happening in your life. Try to pace yourself because you could easily be overloaded by the amount you have on your plate at the moment. Delegate as much work as you can so that you're free to enjoy the incredible buzz you're experiencing. It's all happening!

• Thursday 22 March •

Are you feeling lucky? You'll get lots of enjoyment from the current projects you're involved in today, especially if they have a creative dimension. Your eyes are firmly set on the future, and something that transpires today will take you one step closer to your chosen goal. Someone who believes in you totally will play a major part in your life from now on.

• *Friday 23 March* •

Does a certain someone really mean what they're saying or are they just telling you what they think you want to hear? Be very discerning today because an error of judgment on your part could cost you dear. Perhaps you idealize this person and find it hard to believe that they could deceive you in any way. Be on your guard.

• *Saturday 24 March* •

Today's New Moon gives your confidence a boost, making you feel very sure of yourself and the direction you're heading in. You feel that everything is unfolding in the right way and at the right time. It's also a great opportunity to get together with someone special and do something that you both enjoy. Why not go to the cinema or visit an exhibition?

• *Sunday 25 March* •

Expect the unexpected today because whatever happens is likely to be very different from what you had in mind. If you had planned a relaxing day at home, life will present you with one challenge after another. How you deal with this will determine how well the day goes, but at least you'll be able to see how flexible and unflappable you can be.

• *Monday 26 March* •

It's Monday and, far from having the blues, you're raring to go. It promises to be a lively and active day and you should get plenty of opportunities to both work hard and play hard. Even if you've got a pile of work to do, you'll get through it in no time and still have plenty of energy for socializing. If a certain someone makes a suggestion to go somewhere exotic for a holiday, you'll be sorely tempted. And why not?

• *Tuesday 27 March* •

You're in a wonderfully optimistic and positive mood today, making you feel that anything is possible. Make the most of this expansive frame of mind by doing something that inspires and challenges you to go beyond your usual limits. Whether this is a new perspective, a change of appearance or the letting go of something that has outlived its purpose, you'll benefit enormously from taking the risk.

• *Wednesday 28 March* •

You are pulled in two directions today as your heart and your head vie for supremacy. If you're normally ruled by your head, you might have a hard time letting your feelings take control. On the other hand, if your heart normally calls the shots, you'll be loath to listen to your more rational side as you won't like what it has to say. Try to give both sides an equal voice before you make any decisions.

• *Thursday 29 March* •

It is a pleasure to be with other people today and you'll absolutely delight in the company of one special person. It's a wonderful day for a romance to blossom or an existing relationship to be rekindled, and by the end of the day there'll be enough stars in your eyes to form a galaxy. Friendships are also highly enjoyable – especially your favourite ones. What a wonderful day!

• *Friday 30 March* •

You're in love with love today and in a deliciously affectionate and giving mood. You want to devote time to a loved one and you will tune into their needs. You might even sense what they're feeling intuitively and be able to respond without them even voicing anything. You're also feeling very creative and you might be inspired to write or paint. Give free rein to your imagination and you'll be delighted with the results.

• *Saturday 31 March* •

Get your priorities straight today and ensure that you make time for the things you enjoy. It's a great day for working on a hobby, pastime or anything else that enhances your sense of well-being and happiness. If you've set your heart on something to buy and you're going shopping, don't be surprised if you find something even nicer than what you had in mind.

APRIL AT A GLANCE

Love	♥ ♥ ♥ ♥
Money	£
Career	💻 💻 💻 💻
Health	☼ ☼

• *Sunday 1 April* •

You might not get what you want today but you'll certainly get what you need. You could easily be frustrated by the events that take place, especially if you have set your heart on something and it doesn't come off. Rather than end up feeling frustrated and out of sorts, try to channel this blocked energy into other activities because you could find that it all comes good in the end.

• *Monday 2 April* •

Geminis are renowned for being blessed with enquiring minds and you certainly feel that way at the moment. You'll have the perfect opportunity to increase your understanding of the world in some way today, especially if you're interested in anything mystical or spiritual. You're ready to learn something new that will give your life deeper meaning.

• Tuesday 3 April •

Be prepared to strike out in new directions today and widen your horizons. You have the chance to make an enormous amount of progress if you focus on a long-standing dream or ambition and decide how you could bring it to fruition. You're very keen to show off your talents and skills, and if you can inspire the right people you'll find all the right doors will start to open.

• Wednesday 4 April •

It's a day for asserting yourself. Use your initiative with others, especially if you're leading a team of people. If you need to have a serious talk with a certain someone, don't hold yourself back from saying what you think. Allow yourself to show how strongly you feel about a particular issue, because only then will you – and anyone else concerned – know what really matters to you.

• Thursday 5 April •

You can read a certain someone like a book today, which is just as well as they don't seem to be giving very much away. You're in no doubt that they need some emotional support from you but they're not able to ask for it. Let them know that you're aware of how they're feeling and that you're more than happy to help. It could be exactly what they need to hear.

• Friday 6 April •

Be very selective about the people you spend time with today or you could risk being dumped on in some way. You're in a very sensitive and impressionable mood and you could easily absorb other people's negativity or be on the receiving end of someone's bad temper. Even it means spending time alone, do yourself a favour and avoid anyone you instinctively feel wary of.

• *Saturday 7 April* •

A close personal relationship could hit a brick wall thanks to today's Full Moon. Your only recourse is to discuss your differences and see where you want to go from here. If you both have a list of grievances that there is little chance of resolving, you may need to reconcile yourselves to the fact that it's make or break time.

• *Sunday 8 April* •

It's another challenging day for relationships and you're in no mood to muck about. In fact, you're in a very confrontational frame of mind and you'll have no problems mustering the courage to face up to whatever is currently bothering you. You're determined to tackle any issues that have been swept under the carpet and to get everything out in the open, even if it means a showdown.

• *Monday 9 April* •

The more you can involve yourself in activities that tap into your creative powers, the more fulfilled you will be today. As long as you feel inspired by what you're doing, your powers of concentration will be really strong and you'll screen out anything that doesn't relate to the job in hand. If, on the other hand, what you're doing doesn't engage you, you could feel rather bored and discontented. Is it time for a change?

• *Tuesday 10 April* •

Some very intense emotions stir within you today, and you might try to repress these uncomfortable feelings by doing your best to ignore them. Perhaps they're connected with something – or someone – that you'd rather not think about for whatever reason. But you'll be surprised at how much easier it is to deal with the situation if you stop fighting yourself and simply accept the way you're feeling.

• *Wednesday 11 April* •

You fancy making a few changes to your routine today, especially if your heart sinks at the thought of the day ahead. Consider introducing a more fulfilling element to your daily life because even a small change could make a big difference. Try to spend as much time with friends and loved ones as possible because your batteries will be recharged simply from being in their company.

• *Thursday 12 April* •

It's another day for incorporating something different into your routine and injecting some new life into anything that you feel has gone stale lately. You need freedom of movement and you could easily feel hemmed in if you can't get out and about. If circumstances prevent you from being too adventurous, think of something that would make a positive difference to your life and then promise yourself you will make it happen.

• *Friday 13 April* •

Don't be put off by today's date because you're in a wonderfully dynamic mood and you are all set to sail through the day on a wave of optimism. Why not plan a short break, because you're eager to explore the world and discover new places. Having a rest from current demands and responsibilities will have a marvellously restorative effect and give you the boost you need, especially if you've been running on empty for a while now. Enjoy!

• *Saturday 14 April* •

Are you feeling tired? Perhaps you could go for a long walk and breathe some fresh air. If you've lost your sense of direction recently and have felt rather adrift, now is the time to reorientate yourself and decide how you can best fulfil your aims and ambitions. You've got nothing to lose and everything to gain.

• *Sunday 15 April* •

You're in a very affectionate mood today, and you'll get a big kick out of showing a special loved one how much you care for them. You'll have no difficulty putting words to your feelings because your head and your heart are perfectly in tune. If anything, you might get carried away by the power and depth of your emotions and find yourself waxing lyrical. How romantic!

• *Monday 16 April* •

A certain person knows just how to charm you today and they'll soon have you eating out of their hand. Not that you'll mind – you'll probably love every minute of it! A child or loved one needs to ask you a favour and they know all the right moves to win you over. You can see exactly what they're doing but you'll be only too happy to oblige. Call it positive manipulation!

• *Tuesday 17 April* •

You want to settle down to your responsibilities and duties today, especially if you're in the middle of a business deal or you're planning something really important. There could be some significant developments on the work front, such as someone in authority making you an interesting proposition that could further your career in some way. You're in a strong bargaining position, so ask for what you know you deserve.

• *Wednesday 18 April* •

You're so absorbed in your own thoughts today that you'll be completely oblivious to what others are thinking and feeling. Not exactly the recipe for a harmonious relationship, and sure enough you might run into difficulties with a certain person who interprets your silence as rejection. Making it clear that it's nothing personal and that you need some time to yourself could go a long way to preventing any misunderstandings.

• *Thursday 19 April* •

Keep your own counsel today and don't be swayed by what others say, no matter how convincing they might seem. It's not that anyone is deliberately trying to mislead you, it's just that they might be rather confused and not have their facts straight. Go over anything that you have to sign or agree to in detail, and listen to your gut feelings if something doesn't seem right. Trusting your own judgment will be your best safeguard.

• *Friday 20 April* •

If a relationship has been an uphill struggle recently, you get a chance to put matters to rights today. You're in a very easy-going mood and you'll want to do whatever you can to help things run smoothly. If you're working as part of a team, you'll feel on the same wavelength as everyone else and a strong rapport between you and a colleague could determine the success of a project you're both involved in.

• *Saturday 21 April* •

Today marks a turning point, and any decisions that you make will have a very significant impact on you. Think very carefully about what you really want and be very circumspect about any changes that are in the offing. If you have to sign any legal papers, make sure that you double-check everything for loopholes or hidden pitfalls. An oversight on your part could be more costly than you think.

• *Sunday 22 April* •

During the next two weeks your mind will be drawn to anything of a mystical or spiritual nature. For example, you might want to start studying a subject like psychology or astrology and learn more about what makes you tick. Or you could have an inspiring encounter with someone who thinks in a very different way to you. Whatever happens, your world is about to open up in some new and fascinating ways.

• *Monday 23 April* •

Conserve your energy today because, although you have plenty of mental stamina, you may be somewhat lacking in physical vitality. The New Moon is sensitizing you to your deepest needs and feelings, and you'll be very wrapped up in your innermost thoughts. Although you can't quite put your finger on it yet, you're dimly aware that major change is in the air.

• *Tuesday 24 April* •

It's another day for taking things easy and relaxing as much as possible. Even if you don't get the chance to coast along, at least try to minimize your workload and only do what is absolutely essential. If you can, grab the chance to get out in the fresh air and rejuvenate yourself. It's also an excellent day to make contact with someone with whom you can talk about things that are dear to your heart.

• *Wednesday 25 April* •

Your self-esteem is sky high today, enabling you to put yourself forward or speak up for yourself without any doubt or hesitation. You're in a position to make real progress in every area of your life now, especially if you use your considerable mental powers to determine how you're going to go about it. If you need to do a PR job on yourself, you'll make a big impression.

• *Thursday 26 April* •

Someone in a position of authority could play a very beneficial role in your life today. They might sing your praises and give you a glowing report, or congratulate you on some work that you've done. You could also receive some special acknowledgement from a loved one who can't help but show you how much they care. No wonder you're feeling on top of the world!

• *Friday 27 April* •

You're in the mood to party today, and the more of your favourite people you can gather together the better. You'll want to be with like-minded people so that you can discuss all kinds of interesting topics. Ideally, you should spend time with anyone that you've travelled or studied with, especially if you're planning another trip or you fancy a spirited debate.

• *Saturday 28 April* •

Is money burning a hole in your pocket today? If you've had to curb your spending recently and you're beginning to resent living so thriftily, you might be tempted to splash out and spend some of your hard-earned cash. And why not! Treating yourself to a new outfit or something that makes you feel really good will give you a boost and make all your recent efforts seem worthwhile.

• *Sunday 29 April* •

Today promises to be one of the nicest and most enjoyable days in the whole month. You might get a sudden urge to take off for the day and go somewhere totally new and off the beaten track. Or you could be introduced to someone that you immediately click with and feel as if you've known for years. It's a super day!

• Monday 30 April •

Take care today because you feel torn between doing what is expected of you and following your heart. There's no easy way to resolve this dilemma and you'll need to weigh up the pros and cons of each choice very carefully before you decide what to do. If you need some advice, ask someone who could act as a sounding board but won't influence you one way or the other.

MAY AT A GLANCE

Love	♥ ♥ ♥ ♥ ♥
Money	£
Career	💻 💻 💻
Health	☼ ☼ ☼ ☼

• Tuesday 1 May •

You're firing on all cylinders today and you have the energy and enthusiasm to pursue your goals wholeheartedly. You'll want to be with people who share your vision of the future and who think in an expansive and innovative way. If you suspect that someone is limiting you or holding you back in some way, you'll feel that you have no choice but to move on.

• Wednesday 2 May •

What transpires today leaves you in no doubt about the need to introduce some important changes to a close relationship. Don't expect this person to meet you half-way though.

They're more likely to put up some hefty resistance to any idea of altering the status quo. Use your most persuasive powers of reasoning to talk them into having a frank discussion.

• Thursday 3 May •

Enjoying yourself is high on your list of priorities today. You'll be tempted to give a miss to anything routine and concentrate solely on spending the day with good friends, doing something really entertaining. You might decide to see a show or an exhibition and then splash out on a fabulous meal. Alternatively, you could receive an invitation that would be impossible to turn down.

• Friday 4 May •

You're in a highly motivated frame of mind today and you'll be going full throttle with any project or job that you have to do. You have a strong desire to develop your latent potential, and if you feel that something has been blocking your ability to do this you'll get a special insight into what that is. Once you've identified what's holding you back, you'll progress in leaps and bounds.

• Saturday 5 May •

Certain partnership issues can be resolved today and you might decide to reach a new agreement stipulating what you both need and expect from each other. You may come to the conclusion that it's only by being clear about how you both feel and think that you can hope to have a successful and fulfilling relationship. A friendship that you've always valued will come up trumps and you'll appreciate this person even more.

• Sunday 6 May •

You could listen to someone's sob story today and offer them tea and sympathy. You'll respond with kindness and compassion, and you'll want to do everything you can to help. This could be on a very practical level such as doing some odd jobs, or simply by lending a sympathetic ear and offering some constructive advice. The benefit of your experience will help no end.

• *Monday 7 May* •

Your mind works exceptionally well during the next few weeks, and you will be able to combine your intuitive and analytical qualities to come up with some excellent ideas. Not only will you work at lightning speed and get everything done in next to no time, you'll also be able to tie up a lot of loose ends that have been floating around for ages.

• *Tuesday 8 May* •

If you're happy with the direction you're heading in, you'll want to channel all your energies into your work today and make as much progress as you can. You have an almost limitless supply of stamina and determination to spur you on to greater things. Even if you feel that you haven't yet reached where you want to be, you'll gain a sense of achievement by putting out feelers and letting people know that you're available.

• *Wednesday 9 May* •

You're in the mood for light-hearted company today. You're also feeling very magnanimous, and if there's someone in your life that you'd love to spoil you'll do everything you can to make them feel special. If you're feeling flush, you might decide to treat yourself to a long weekend away somewhere beautiful and luxurious. You deserve a treat!

• *Thursday 10 May* •

You'll take great pleasure in doing something creative or artistic today. Try to set aside some time for a favourite pastime or hobby that uplifts you, or listen to some inspiring music. Ideally, you'll want to have some time alone in order to put your thoughts together, but if that simply isn't possible, give yourself a few minutes of quiet time before you go to sleep. You'll feel much more at peace if you do.

• *Friday 11 May* •

If you're normally blessed with confidence and self-assurance, you'll wonder what's happened today. You could be seized with an attack of shyness, making you reluctant to speak up or stand your ground. Or someone might try to intimidate you with the sheer force of their personality. It may be a good idea to step back for a while and regroup before returning to the fray.

• *Saturday 12 May* •

Steer clear of anyone who never has a kind word to say because you're very sensitive to criticism today. A certain someone might discover your Achilles heel and exploit the fact that you're feeling vulnerable, or they could judge you too harshly, making you want to withdraw and lick your wounds. Discuss the way you're feeling with a good friend that you know you can trust.

• *Sunday 13 May* •

You're fizzing with energy today and you'll want to let off steam and liven things up by letting your hair down and having fun. You might feel inspired to do something unconventional or totally original just to be different, and you'll hanker to be with people who share your sense of adventure. Whatever you do, you'll want it to be breathtaking, exciting and memorable.

• *Monday 14 May* •

You feel on very solid ground today and you will command respect and admiration for whatever you say or do. You have both the clout and the authority to promote yourself and your ideas, and you'll impress others with your expertise and experience. It's also a good day to get on top of your finances and you'll gain a great deal of satisfaction from putting all your affairs in order.

• *Tuesday 15 May* •

Someone may step out of line and try your patience today, making for rather a tense atmosphere between you. Keeping the lid on your feelings will only intensify them, so if you want to clear the air and resolve the discord you'd be better off saying what has aggravated you. If you're going out with friends you could meet someone you feel strongly attracted to, but are they a good bet for a relationship? Look before you leap!

• *Wednesday 16 May* •

If you're tired of wearing the same sorts of clothes or you are fed up with the colour of your hair, you'll want to find new ways to enhance your appearance today. You're feeling bold and confident enough to change your image and you'll want to create a new look that reflects the more extrovert side of your personality. Trust your own judgment when choosing your new image and you can't go wrong.

• *Thursday 17 May* •

Make sure that you're on the ball today if you're dealing with people in authority because they might take you by surprise in some way. It's one of those days when nothing is what it seems and you can't count on anything going according to plan. Even the simplest tasks could end up taxing your brain and trying your patience. Console yourself by arranging something to look forward to at the end of the day.

• *Friday 18 May* •

A certain person stirs your passions today and you'll be irresistibly attracted to them in a way that you could find disconcerting and somewhat overwhelming. Your first reaction might be to play for time in order to get your emotions under control, but no amount of rational thinking is likely to put out the fire that is threatening to consume you. Talk about hot stuff!

• *Saturday 19 May* •

The weekend ahead promises to be deliciously romantic, and one that you'll remember for many years to come. Whether you've just met someone or you've been together for a while, your love life is blossoming and you'll feel very loving and affectionate towards you-know-who. You could also have a surprise in store that will make you feel like the happiest person alive. Sounds good!

• *Sunday 20 May* •

You're eager to squeeze as much enjoyment from all your activities as possible and you'll want to fill your day with love, laughter and happiness. It's a wonderful time to take off and do something on the spur of the moment with a special person. You might feel like getting in the car and going where the fancy takes you, or you may decide to visit one of your favourite places. Whatever you do, you'll have a ball.

• *Monday 21 May* •

You want to spend as much time as possible with friends and loved ones today, especially if you can have a cosy get-together and share your thoughts and feelings. You could feel a strong rapport with one particular person and you might even have telepathic communication with each other. Even if you haven't known each other for long, the link you have today will make you feel as if you've been friends forever.

• *Tuesday 22 May* •

Today's New Moon indicates that you're embarking on a new chapter in your life. You're ready to make certain changes and you'll find it easier to explain your needs to those that matter most. You'll also be more receptive and open to what others require from you, making your relationships more nurturing and supportive. However, don't demand from others more than you're prepared to give yourself.

• *Wednesday 23 May* •

You're on great form today, full of vitality and self-confidence. It's an excellent day to show off your talents and abilities. Your enthusiasm and easy-going manner will make a very good impression and if you have to do any entertaining that's work-related it's bound to be a great success. This is one of those occasions when business and pleasure do mix and everyone has a great time.

• *Thursday 24 May* •

Don't be surprised if communications go haywire today and anything electrical starts to play up. Phones and computers could go on the blink and letters might get lost in the post. Take extra care if you have to send anything important in case it goes missing, and make sure that there's no room for any misunderstandings between you and others. Apart from that, there's absolutely nothing to worry about!

• *Friday 25 May* •

Things are still not running smoothly and you could experience a minor setback or delay that will slow everything down for a while. To say that steam will be coming out of your ears is an understatement, but try to counteract your frustration by concentrating on a task that will take your mind off the current difficulties. At least that way you won't feel as if you've wasted the whole day.

• Saturday 26 May •

Has someone got the hump? You might feel like giving a loved one a wide berth today as they're giving off distinctly hostile vibes. The problem is that they may say something that you find particularly wounding and hard to shrug off. They'll soon realize that they owe you an apology and you'll no doubt find it in your heart to forgive them.

• Sunday 27 May •

Thank goodness yesterday's contretemps is behind you! You're in the mood to have a good laugh with close friends. You might feel like letting off steam by taking a long walk or doing some kind of sport. The accent is firmly on fun but don't be surprised if your competitive streak emerges and you get a real kick from pitting your physical or mental prowess against someone else's.

• Monday 28 May •

You're at your most outgoing, vibrant and confident today, and anyone who's lucky enough to spend time with you will thoroughly enjoy your company. Your sparkling wit and positive attitude will have a wonderfully uplifting effect on others, and one person in particular will benefit from being around you. Perhaps they've been down in the dumps recently and something you say cheers them up no end.

• Tuesday 29 May •

Anything that seems too restrictive or predictable will get you down today, so do things that add variety and interest to your life. You may not be able to avoid a certain amount of routine, but if you're a typical Gemini you'll probably find something to take your mind off the drudgery. You might need to lend an ear to someone with a tale of woe and give them some helpful advice.

• *Wednesday 30 May* •

It's an excellent day to concentrate on your priorities in life and decide how you can make more time for them. You may have realized that the things you most enjoy and which give you the greatest joy and happiness are not always at the top of your priority list, so you now want to redress the balance. It's also a good time to review your finances and see how to make your money work better for you.

• *Thursday 31 May* •

You're in a very sociable and gregarious mood today and you'll enjoy mixing with all kinds of people, especially if there's something different or unusual about them. You might also feel like getting in touch with people that you haven't seen recently. If you haven't got anything exciting lined up for the weekend, see what ideas you can come up with.

JUNE AT A GLANCE

Love	♥ ♥ ♥ ● ♥
Money	£ $ £ $ £
Career	💻 💻 💻 💻 💻
Health	☼ ☼ ☼ ☼ ☼

• *Friday 1 June* •

There's an emotionally charged atmosphere between you and a loved one today, making you feel as if you're riding a roller-coaster. You may have a strong desire to relate more deeply to this person but this could bring up some uncomfortable feelings in you. If you can accept that you are in emotional conflict, you'll have a much better chance of coming to terms with how you're feeling.

• *Saturday 2 June* •

Thank goodness yesterday's rather tense atmosphere has now blown away. Today you're able to draw closer to your other half and this will be very beneficial for your relationship. It's a terrific chance to spend a few days together and do something that you both enjoy, especially if that means getting away and simply enjoying one another's company. Pick somewhere beautiful and peaceful.

• *Sunday 3 June* •

If you need to say something important, you'll find exactly the right words to express how you're feeling. In fact, you can make up for any recent misunderstandings or tricky communications by opening your heart and letting a certain someone know how much you care. This will bring you the closeness that you've been longing for.

• *Monday 4 June* •

Even your best-laid plans could come unstuck until late June. Your computer may pack up or you could have difficulties getting through to people. If you have to send anything important through the post, take precautionary steps to make sure that nothing goes astray. If you become rather absent-minded and forget things, it might help to write yourself notes – preferably in duplicate!

• *Tuesday 5 June* •

Your social plans could go awry today because of an annoying mistake or misunderstanding. You might arrange to meet someone at a certain time and place and wait for ages before realizing you should be somewhere else. You may take these confusing situations in your stride normally but this time you're much more likely to overreact and get yourself into a state.

• *Wednesday 6 June* •

You're in no mood to let the grass grow under your feet today and you're determined to put your formidable energy to good use. It's an excellent day to fight for what you believe in and stand up for yourself. Daring to speak out on any issues that are important will certainly make people sit up and listen, and the power of your convictions could win someone over to your way of thinking.

• *Thursday 7 June* •

During the next four weeks you'll derive great pleasure from working on a hobby or pastime. You're at your most creative and you could discover a new gift or talent. If you have already found an outlet for your creativity, you'll want to develop your abilities even further now. Being surrounded by nature will fill you with energy, as well as giving you a sense of peace and well-being.

• *Friday 8 June* •

Think carefully about what you would like to achieve today and then go all out to make it happen. You'll have every opportunity to clinch something that you've been working towards, and you'll feel a tremendous sense of satisfaction and fulfilment when you reach your goal. A boss or authority figure is about to recognize your potential and give you the chance to prove your worth, so take centre stage and shine!

• *Saturday 9 June* •

You'll really enjoy someone's lively and stimulating company today and you may happily spend all day exchanging ideas and opinions. Whoever this person is, they have a wonderfully uplifting and energizing effect on you, and their intelligent and thought-provoking conversation will really sharpen your wits. A strange or unusual coincidence sets you thinking about the connections between you. Intriguing!

• Sunday 10 June •

Dreaming of foreign lands? You're in a world of your own today and your thoughts might turn to a holiday that you're really looking forward to. If you still haven't booked anything, you might see a travel programme on television or read an article in the paper that inspires you to visit somewhere far-flung and exotic. Somehow the thought of sticking to the tried and tested path holds no appeal and you're ready to respond to the call for adventure!

• Monday 11 June •

You'll feel happiest when working behind the scenes today or left to your own devices. You'll achieve a lot more if there are no distractions around you and you can focus on the job in hand to the exclusion of everything and everyone else. You're also in the mood to have some time to yourself and get your thoughts in order, especially if you need to have a serious talk with a certain someone.

• Tuesday 12 June •

This is an excellent day to think about how well you're taking care of yourself and whether you need to make any changes to your lifestyle. Perhaps your diet could be improved or you should be taking more rest. If so, don't put off until tomorrow what you can do today. Getting expert advice might be one good way of starting as you mean to go on.

• Wednesday 13 June •

The pace of your work really heats up today and it looks as if certain demands will be made of you. A boss or superior is in a particularly critical mood and nothing seems to be good enough for them. Try to keep out of their way as much as possible if you want to avoid any sharp remarks or negative comments, and do your best to get everything done as well and efficiently as possible, even if that means working over-time. It will be worth it.

• *Thursday 14 June* •

What a delightfully optimistic and sunny mood you're in today! It makes a lovely change from yesterday and you're eager to get out and stretch your wings. Even if you don't have the whole day to roam around at your leisure, make time for at least one pleasurable pursuit. If money is burning a hole in your pocket, you'll have a wonderful time treating yourself to something really special.

• *Friday 15 June* •

Life is full of wonderful opportunities today and you'll be keen to explore some of them, especially if there's a romantic element involved. It's an especially good day for being with an intimate partner or making it a priority to get out and meet someone new. If you're a single Gemini, you could meet someone you feel madly attracted to, even though they aren't your usual type. Who cares?

• *Saturday 16 June* •

Talk about get up and go! You've got so much energy today that it will be hard to keep up with you. If you have to tackle any jobs around the house or garden, you'll attack them with tremendous gusto. Not that you're planning on working all day long because you'll throw yourself into any social activities with the same level of dynamism and enthusiasm. Move over, Speedy Gonzalez!

• *Sunday 17 June* •

You're drawn to unusual people and places today, and you'll want to experience as much variety as you can. You might be invited somewhere you've never been to before and be absolutely fascinated and enchanted by it. Or you could be introduced to someone from a different background or culture to yours and feel as though your whole world has opened up as a result. You'll be in your element.

● *Monday 18 June* ●

Any group activities will go down well today and you'll really enjoy being with people who are on the same wavelength as you. Someone may help you by pulling a few strings on your behalf, or you could hear that you've been elected to a position you've been aspiring to for a while. It's also a very auspicious time for starting a new venture that will take you in a different direction.

● *Tuesday 19 June* ●

Life continues to feel exciting today and you'll have no time for anything that feels dreary or routine. Your mind is working overtime and you'll be bombarded with new insights about yourself and the world around you. You might come across a book or an article that stimulates your interest in exploring your personality in more depth. Not only that, you'll also want to discover and learn more about the people who are close to you.

● *Wednesday 20 June* ●

You're full of high hopes today and determined to make everything work out for the best. If you're currently experiencing a difficulty with a partner or loved one, you'll suddenly be filled with the confidence to tackle the issues that are standing between you. You intuitively feel that the only way to deal with this is by being open, and that the more honest you are, the easier it will be to clear the air.

• *Thursday 21 June* •

Today's New Moon is making you more aware of your security needs. If you've been trying to conserve your cash but haven't been able to find a viable way of doing it, this would be a good time to get some expert advice on savings and investments. You might also want to think about your emotional well-being and decide what will make you feel more secure. Promise yourself to do something about it.

• *Friday 22 June* •

It's a day for conserving your energy because you don't have as much stamina as usual. Taking more on than you can comfortably handle will wear you out both emotionally and physically, as well as undermining your confidence, so do yourself a favour and only do what's manageable. Ask a good friend for help if you feel in need of support. That's what they're there for!

• *Saturday 23 June* •

Over the next few days you'll be concerned with the image you present to the world and how you could make a stronger impact. For instance, you may decide to alter the way you look to reflect another facet of your personality, or you may want to change an aspect of your behaviour so you make more of an impression. Give yourself time to mull over these ideas because what seems like a good idea today may lose its appeal tomorrow.

• *Sunday 24 June* •

You're feeling on top of the world and you'll want to inject as much excitement into your day as possible. A plan for the future looks like being a success, especially if you think big and confidently assume that everything will turn out well. If you're going away for the weekend or on a longer trip, you'll have the time of your life. Bon voyage!

• *Monday 25 June* •

You're in a compassionate and affectionate mood today and you'll have no difficulty reassuring someone who's feeling insecure or left out in the cold. Perhaps you haven't had as much time for them as you would have liked recently, but at least now you can make amends and give them all the TLC they need. Why not treat yourselves and go out for a special meal to one of your favourite places?

• *Tuesday 26 June* •

Are you feeling moody or is someone else blowing hot and cold? You might need to put your emotions under the microscope today to find out how you really feel about a certain someone. Perhaps you're ambivalent and you don't want to admit it, or are you on the receiving end of some mixed messages? Either way, it's time to do some detective work and get to the bottom of things.

• *Wednesday 27 June* •

Partnerships continue to come under the spotlight, and you'll want to channel lots of energy into your one-to-one relationships. Establishing a good rapport with your nearest and dearest is very important to you, but resist the temptation of trying to force any issues or coming on too strong. Watch your tendency to become impatient, as it will only complicate matters.

• *Thursday 28 June* •

Thank goodness communications begin to return to normal today, and with luck things should start to run more smoothly. Be wary of putting all your eggs in one basket at the moment because you could be closing yourself off to other, more promising, options. Hold back and see what comes to you rather than trying to make things happen.

• *Friday 29 June* •

Get set to roll up your sleeves and work hard today. If you decide what you want to achieve and how you're going to go about it, you'll make excellent progress. This is the perfect opportunity to show colleagues and clients that you've got what it takes, especially if you've been hiding your light under a bushel recently.

• *Saturday 30 June* •

Any feelings of restriction or limitation that have been nagging away at you could come to the surface today, making you feel extremely restless. If you honestly feel that something or someone is holding you back, you'll need to be honest with yourself and take the appropriate action. Whether this is a radical move or simply a readjustment, you can no longer ignore the urge for change.

JULY AT A GLANCE

Love	❤ ❤ ❤ ❤ ❤
Money	£ $ £ $ £
Career	💻 💻
Health	☼ ☼ ☼ ☼

• *Sunday 1 July* •

You're prepared to give someone the benefit of the doubt today, especially over anything connected with work. This will be a very positive and constructive move because you'll win both their trust and respect. It's also a good time to get some medical advice on any health concerns that you have. If any of your symptoms are stress-related, try to find more time to relax and unwind.

• *Monday 2 July* •

What a productive day! You're in the mood to streamline your life and it's time to think about getting rid of anything that's past its sell-by date. If there's anyone from your past that you feel you've outgrown or no longer have anything in common with, you may decide that you need to leave them behind now and move on.

• *Tuesday 3 July* •

Your emotions run deep today and you'll feel things most intensely in intimate partnerships. You have a strong urge to reach out to others and show them how much you care about them. However, don't be too dismayed if a certain someone doesn't reciprocate or match the strength of your feelings. It's probably because your demonstrative mood comes as a complete surprise to them.

• *Wednesday 4 July* •

Got itchy feet? Life becomes very adventurous and exciting today and you'll be really keen to explore pastures new. If you're setting off on holiday this month, you'll be counting the days and thinking about all the fun things you've got planned. Even if you're not about to take off, you're in the mood to broaden your mental horizons. Being in stimulating company would do the trick.

• *Thursday 5 July* •

Today's Full Moon brings some very personal issues to the fore and it might be time to tell a certain someone a few home truths. For instance, you might not be happy with the way your joint finances are managed, especially if you seem to be bearing the brunt of the daily expenses. They won't necessarily like what you have to say, but at least you'll get the chance to resolve your differences.

• Friday 6 July •

Get ready for some exciting new developments during the next three weeks. This is particularly good news if you've been far too modest because you'll really begin to shine now. Making yourself more visible will give you a chance to show off your skills and abilities and gain the recognition you deserve. All this will do wonders for your confidence and self-esteem.

• Saturday 7 July •

You're on sparkling form right now and you'll be the life and soul of any social gathering that you're invited to. You also have some great ideas that you want to discuss with others, or you could be very excited about a plan which could radically change the way you live. A completely different side of your personality could come out today, which will take a certain someone by surprise. Didn't they realize you're a Gemini?

• Sunday 8 July •

You have the courage of your convictions today, especially if that means defending your beliefs. Anything that smacks of injustice will really rattle you, and you'll be very vociferous in defending your position. You may also want to fight someone else's battle, especially if you feel that they've been hard done by or are unable to stand up for themselves.

• Monday 9 July •

This is a good day to think about your life and try to find ways to create more free time. You may be feeling trapped in too tight a schedule and decide that you need more of a balance between work and play. Once you've worked out how to give yourself more space, you'll find that everything else naturally falls into place.

• *Tuesday 10 July* •

Everything you do goes well today and you'll automatically attract the support that you need. The focus is very much on your standing in the world and, providing you've laid the groundwork, you'll feel a great sense of achievement. You might meet someone who will play a very important role in your career and be enormously beneficial to you, in more ways than one.

• *Wednesday 11 July* •

Feel like partying? You bet you do! You're in a delightfully self-indulgent mood today and you'll enjoy nothing better than having a good time eating and drinking with friends. A night on the town could be just what you need because it will give you the chance to unwind. Besides which, you're too dis-tracted at the moment to put all your energies into work, and having fun will give you a real lift.

• *Thursday 12 July* •

Your intuition is spot on today and you'll be able to act on your hunches with total confidence. You'll also find it easy to express your emotions in a very sensitive and seductive way. No one is immune to your charm and allure at the moment, least of all a certain person that you've got your eye on. Let's face it, they don't stand a chance of resisting your sexual magnetism – and why would they want to!

• *Friday 13 July* •

Don't worry about the date because today signals the start of a very positive and promising new cycle in your life. In the coming weeks and months you'll have every opportunity to develop and expand your self-worth and acquire more con-fidence in yourself. You'll also be able to increase your earning potential as well as gaining more recognition for your gifts and abilities. Congratulations!

• *Saturday 14 July* •

You're torn between erring on the side of caution and taking a risk today. Your carefree side feels inspired to drop everything and do something out of the ordinary, while the more down-to-earth part of you would rather play it safe and stick to what's familiar. Although you'll try to use your powers of reasoning to decide which path to take, in the end you may simply have to go with your impulses.

• *Sunday 15 July* •

If you have to pay a pile of bills and sort out other money matters, this is a good time to get everything in order. It may not be the most exciting task but at least you're in the right mood to get all your paperwork out of the way. If you're going on holiday soon, check that you have everything you need, including all the right documentation. It will save a last-minute panic.

• *Monday 16 July* •

Someone is feeling very volatile today and they could easily fly off the handle if they don't like what they hear or are offended by a comment. It won't make your life any easier if you happen to be on the receiving end of their outburst, and you may be tempted to respond in kind and give as good as you get. If you do, something could be said that you both end up regretting.

• *Tuesday 17 July* •

Your nose could be put out of joint today by someone who tries to challenge your authority. Perhaps one of the family is testing you to see how far they can go and how much they can get away with. Or someone at work may try to undermine your position in some way, making you feel vulnerable and insecure. Do your best to stand firm and let it be known that you're no pushover.

• *Wednesday 18 July* •

You could be swept off your feet by a sudden surge of passion today and your normal capacity to concentrate will temporarily desert you. Your feelings are paramount at the moment, so you might as well give them a free rein and stop trying to stay in control. If you have a 'Do Not Disturb' sign handy, you'll probably want to hang it on the bedroom door!

• *Thursday 19 July* •

It's all systems go today and you'll really enjoy yourself if you can go exploring somewhere or expand your mental horizons in some way. You feel infused with a tremendous amount of energy and you'll want to make plans, especially if they involve taking off with a loved one for a few days. Forget trying to knuckle down to any kind of hard work right now because you're simply not in the mood.

• *Friday 20 July* •

Your emotions have never been very far from the surface recently and today is no different. Your feelings are very intense, especially where your love life is concerned, and you'll want to immerse yourself in an intimate relationship. The fact that you're feeling so passionate about things could work against you if you have any kind of disagreement as you're likely to get very hot under the collar.

• *Saturday 21 July* •

You are thinking very creatively today about ways to increase your income and you'll have no shortage of brainwaves. You're about to discover how resourceful you are when you put your mind to it, and the more positive you are about your ability to make things happen, the more likely you are to get what you ask for. Think big and expect the best!

• *Sunday 22 July* •

You're full of joy and optimism today and you'll want to enjoy the company of loved ones. You may have something to celebrate, in which case you'll really want to go to town and make it a very special occasion. It is delightfully easy to get on with everyone and it's an ideal time to establish a stronger rapport with someone dear to your heart. Now, who could that be?

• *Monday 23 July* •

Communication is never a problem at the best of times for Geminis, but today you'll take the art of speaking your mind to a new level. Whether you're selling something or expressing an opinion, it will be hard not to get carried away by your infectious enthusiasm for your subject. Someone might be so enthusiastic about one of your ideas or schemes that they'll be willing to put their money where their mouth is before you know it. Well done!

• *Tuesday 24 July* •

You probably prefer being at home today than out in the world. You'll get great pleasure from throwing yourself into any creative jobs that need doing around the house, especially if you can enjoy the immediate benefits of your handiwork. You might decide to do some gardening or a spot of painting to brighten things up. If you have the place to yourself, you'll really enjoy your own company.

• *Wednesday 25 July* •

One friendship in particular brings you a lot of happiness today. Someone may prove that they're no fair-weather friend by offering you emotional or financial support, and you'll realize how blessed you are to have them in your life. By the same token, you may also want to devote yourself to someone in need and give them a helping hand in whatever way you can.

• *Thursday 26 July* •

If you need to confide in someone today, you'll find them very approachable and helpful. Not only will they listen carefully and give you their considered opinion, they might even offer a solution or give you a new perspective that clarifies everything for you. You could get involved in a stimulating and light-hearted debate about a subject that you love talking about. Will anyone else get a word in edgeways?

• *Friday 27 July* •

Take it easy today because you could be feeling under par. Your energy levels are quite low and you'll need to pace yourself and not bite off more than you can chew. You might also feel rather irritable with a colleague or partner, especially if you keep pushing yourself and get worn out. If you listen to your body and rest when you need to, you'll soon bounce back.

• *Saturday 28 July* •

You're in danger of getting locked into a battle of wills today, with neither party being willing to back down. The problem is that both you and a certain someone believe that right is on your side, and nothing that the other says or does makes a scrap of difference. If you don't want to spend the whole day stuck in a power struggle, perhaps you need to declare a truce.

• *Sunday 29 July* •

After yesterday's fall-out, you feel more retiring and reserved today. Listening to music, reading poetry or simply allowing your thoughts to wander is all you want to do. You're not interested in dealing with life's harsh realities, and you'd far rather drift off into the world of your imagination. If you can spend some time in a beauty spot, you'll feel renewed and revitalized.

• *Monday 30 July* •

Your ability to see the bigger picture is enhanced today because you're in a very thoughtful and philosophical frame of mind. Being on your own and giving yourself a chance to think about what's really important to you will be very beneficial, especially if you feel that you need to make certain changes. Don't be afraid to confront an unpleasant issue – you'll feel as if you've unburdened yourself.

• *Tuesday 31 July* •

You're feeling very restless today and you'll be much happier if you can get out and about. If you have to stay put, the best way to counteract any boredom is to keep your mind occupied and stimulated. Find something that really absorbs you and you'll soon feel much more at ease. You could hear from someone that you haven't seen for ages. That will cheer you up!

AUGUST AT A GLANCE

Love	♥ ♥ ♥
Money	£ $ £ $ £
Career	💻 💻
Health	☼ ☼

• *Wednesday 1 August* •

You are eager to assert yourself today, and your determination alone will ensure that you make a great deal of progress. You're a veritable dynamo right now and you'll leave no stone unturned in your quest to make your mark and establish yourself in the minds of others. Just be careful that you don't get on the wrong side of someone who has the power to scupper your plans, because a setback at this stage could really upset things.

• *Thursday 2 August* •

You'd better mind your P's and Q's today, otherwise you could end up saying the wrong thing and upsetting a partner or loved one. On the other hand, you may want to be deliberately provocative in order to get something out into the open. Perhaps you feel that things are being swept under the carpet, and unless you confront the issue nothing will be resolved. Think carefully about how to tackle this situation and try not to get bogged down in recriminations.

• *Friday 3 August* •

You're determined to do things in style today, and you won't want to be restricted by any nitty-gritty details. You're much more interested in the bigger picture and being involved in the more creative aspects of things than attending to any practical considerations. That's all well and good, but if you really want to make a big impact, you must make sure that everything is taken care of. Delegate if necessary.

• *Saturday 4 August* •

You may be forced to question certain assumptions or re-evaluate your behaviour today. Perhaps you need to think about how much time and energy you devote to a close relationship, especially if things have been strained recently. The Full Moon is making you more aware of where you can bring greater balance into your life, as well as helping you to be more objective about getting some of your needs met.

• *Sunday 5 August* •

You're feeling very affectionate towards others today and you'll want to let loved ones know how much you appreciate them. You also feel like having some fun, and your current enthusiasm means you'll have no difficulty in getting people to join you. If you're going to a gathering or party today, you could bump into someone that you find extremely attractive. That'll put a twinkle in your eye!

• Monday 6 August •

It's a fabulous day to treat yourself, especially if it's going to enhance your sense of well-being in some way. You might be tempted to have a wonderfully sensual massage or some other luxurious beauty treatment. Alternatively, you might decide to take yourself off to your favourite restaurant and indulge yourself with some delicious food. You could also get a big boost when you hear some very good news about a financial matter.

• Tuesday 7 August •

You're feeling very energetic and positive today, and it looks as if something really nice is going to happen. It's a day for surprises, and some unexpected news will really make your spirits soar and give you something to celebrate. You'll be in your element in any kind of social situation and you'll rise to the occasion if you have to speak in front of a group of people. What a wonderful day!

• Wednesday 8 August •

Your intuition is working at full throttle today, giving you an uncanny ability to know what others are thinking. This will be enormously helpful at work because it'll keep you one step ahead, as well as keeping everyone else guessing. You may also spot an opportunity that no one else notices, which will give you a chance to put yourself forward. Any ideas for promoting yourself are worth capitalizing on now, as are your talents and abilities.

• Thursday 9 August •

Everything looks set to go smoothly today and you have every confidence that whatever you put your energies into will have a positive outcome. You're feeling very strong and independent, and you'll want to go your own way as much as possible without being hampered or slowed down by anyone or anything. Try to be diplomatic if you're telling a certain someone that you need breathing space at the moment.

• *Friday 10 August* •

It's a day to explore new situations and enjoy meeting like-minded people. You're raring to go at the moment, and you need to direct your energies out into the world and share your sense of excitement with others. You'll be amazed by how inspired you feel when you get together with other stimulating minds and share your ideas. A whole new perspective is about to unfold in front of you!

• *Saturday 11 August* •

You're very receptive to the moods of others today and there's one person in particular that you'll want to spoil and make a fuss of. Perhaps they're feeling under the weather and in need of lots of care and attention, or maybe they need to talk about something that's bothering them. Either way, you'll be the soul of sympathy and will do your best to cheer them up.

• *Sunday 12 August* •

All quiet on the home front? Not for long, because someone is being very volatile and outspoken today. This could be a family member who's in danger of flying off the handle or you might be the one who's about to blow your top. Either way, creating a scene isn't going to sort out your differences and will probably make things worse than they are already. Try to release the tension without going OTT.

• *Monday 13 August* •

Although you're not feeling quite as energetic as you have been recently, you're still amazingly full of life and keen to tackle whatever is on the agenda today. Having said that, it could be a difficult day to plan ahead because, just when you think you're heading one way, there will be a sudden and unforeseen change of direction. At least you can't complain that life is boring!

● *Tuesday 14 August* ●

If you're under a lot of pressure at work at the moment, try to find a time in the day to let off steam and relax. Getting through to a boss or authority figure could feel like hitting your head against a brick wall, and it will only undermine your confidence. You'd be far better off taking a back seat for a while and doing something that doesn't frustrate you.

● *Wednesday 15 August* ●

If you need to do some DIY jobs at home, use the next couple of weeks to get these out of the way. You'll gain a lot of satisfaction from doing anything useful around the house, particularly if everything runs more efficiently as a result. You're also in a creative mood and you'll really enjoy picking out colours for home furnishings or paints. It looks like being quite a productive fortnight.

● *Thursday 16 August* ●

You're full of creative ideas today, so find plenty of outlets to express them. You'll have a marvellous opportunity to take the initiative and get a new project off the ground, especially if it's going to alter or improve your base of operations. Luck could arrive in unexpected ways. If you're about to get married or start a family, you're all set for success!

● *Friday 17 August* ●

Is it a case of absence makes the heart grow fonder or out of sight out of mind? Your feelings for a certain person are going through some fundamental changes and you need time today to rethink your relationship. The problem is that you're not in a very decisive mood and you are prone to changing your mind every now and then. Wait until you are clearer about how you feel before you make any decisions.

• *Saturday 18 August* •

Fun-loving and frivolous are the two words that best describe your current mood, and you want to make the most of your free time this weekend. Do anything that will bring you pleasure because not only will you enjoy yourself, you'll also bring a lot of joy and happiness to others as well. If there's anything in your diary that you really don't feel like doing, see if you can put it off for another time. You want to please yourself.

• *Sunday 19 August* •

If you've been overindulging recently and it's beginning to show, this is a good day to start doing something about it. You might read an article that inspires you to become fitter by taking another approach to the way you eat and exercise. Or a friend might recommend a food supplement or some vitamins to give you a more balanced diet. You're ready to take yourself in hand, and what better time than the present?

• *Monday 20 August* •

You could feel rather frayed around the edges today if people at work are placing too many demands on you. Maybe you feel that you don't have enough freedom to do things your way and you are hampered by the constraints that are being put upon you. Let others know how you're feeling and see if you can come to an arrangement that gives you more autonomy.

• *Tuesday 21 August* •

It's another day where you're likely to feel up against it, as others seem unable or unwilling to see things from your point of view. Are you sure that you're not doing anything to exacerbate the problem? If not, then you need to carry on standing your ground and refusing to agree to anything that you don't feel right about. You may need to cut your losses if you can't reach a mutual agreement.

• *Wednesday 22 August* •

You want to do something uplifting that will recharge your batteries today, especially if you're feeling rather flat or deflated after the events of the last few days. A friend or loved one will be a tower of strength and give you moral support as well as the pleasure of their company. You'll soon bounce back to your normal energy levels, ready to face the world again. Good for you!

• *Thursday 23 August* •

Take time out today to reflect on your needs, especially if you still feel that you need to restructure a fundamental aspect of your life. Your emotions are quite stirred up by a current situation, making it difficult for you to assess things rationally. Try to be guided by your instincts and let them tell you how best to proceed from here. You'll be amazed by the strength of your intuition at the moment.

• *Friday 24 August* •

You're full of brilliant ideas on how to improve your situation, but don't divulge anything until you've got a watertight plan and you know exactly what you want to say. Playing your cards close to your chest will arouse a certain someone's curiosity and you may feel tempted to confide in them. But make sure their motives aren't suspect and that they really are on your side.

• *Saturday 25 August* •

Matters of the heart take a turn for the better today and you'll want to get very close to you-know-who, both emotionally and physically. Your feelings are very intense and passionate, and you exude a strong sexual energy, making your partner very responsive to the signals you're sending out. They may not be the only one, and you could have to reject any unwanted attention kindly but firmly.

• *Sunday 26 August* •

There's no point in trying to put your life into perspective at the moment because there's far too much going on for you to gain a true picture. If you're feeling daunted and overwhelmed by it all, why not get out and have some fun today? Not only will it be a welcome distraction, it will also give your mind a chance to stop thinking for a while.

• *Monday 27 August* •

This is a great day to get your ideas across, because others are very receptive and supportive. It's also a wonderful day for getting together with some special people and doing something life-affirming. You might decide to go out for the day to a beautiful and inspiring place. Or if you feel like taking a mental journey, you might invest in some new books that are spiritually uplifting.

• *Tuesday 28 August* •

The astrological focus is on your finances today and it's an ideal time to make them as safe and as solid as possible. Financial security is an important issue at the moment and you want to make sure that your money is working well for you. Maybe it's time for you to become more self-sufficient or to start thinking about ways to increase your earning power? If you want to invest some cash, shop around for the best savings policies.

• *Wednesday 29 August* •

You feel very grounded and realistic about your options today. You'll want to weigh up the pros and cons of any decisions that you have to make, especially if they concern a joint partnership. You're prepared to work hard to sort out any differences between you and a colleague or loved one. Once you've resolved the practicalities, everything else will fall into place.

• *Thursday 30 August* •

Rest assured that you have the respect and admiration of those who are important to you. You have a clear vision of where you're going and how you can change a situation for the better. Your campaign to improve the status quo will have a very beneficial effect on your relationship with others, particularly any close relatives with whom you've had difficulties in the past.

• *Friday 31 August* •

You impress others with your knowledge and expertise today and this will stand you in very good stead for the future. Dare to show yourself in your true light and you'll get a very positive response from both colleagues and clients, not to mention someone closer to home. On a personal level, you might reveal an aspect of your character that you normally restrain, with stunning results!

SEPTEMBER AT A GLANCE

Love	♥ ♥ ♥ ♥ ♥
Money	£ $ £
Career	💻
Health	☼

• *Saturday 1 September* •

You have your own very distinct views on how you would like to spend today and you're not in the mood to compromise. The problem is that others also have their own ideas about what they'd like to do, so it seems inevitable that you're on course for a disagreement. How you ultimately resolve your differences will depend on someone being willing to back down. Who's it going to be?

• *Sunday 2 September* •

It's another day for frayed tempers and charged emotions, and the Full Moon brings unresolved domestic differences to a head. You could be tempted to ignore the root cause of the current discord between you and a loved one, hoping that it will sort itself out. Or you can decide to get to the heart of the matter by telling each other how you really feel. Spending more time together may be all that's needed to get you back on an even keel.

• *Monday 3 September* •

If you've done a lot of talking recently you'll feel like some peace and quiet today. What most appeals to you is spending a low-key day doing something that doesn't require any effort on your part. If you're busy at work, you'll probably welcome the distraction as it will be a respite from all the recent emotional ups and downs. Once you've recharged your batteries, you'll feel ready to live life to the full again.

• *Tuesday 4 September* •

Draw yourself up to your full height today because it's the ideal time to make your mark at work and show others how indispensable you are. You're filled with a sense of your own worth and you'll want to be acknowledged for what you do. You could be offered greater powers of responsibility and the opportunity to become more of a key player and have a bigger role to play, not to mention a larger pay packet. Congratulations!

• *Wednesday 5 September* •

You're feeling very positive and optimistic today, and determined to make the best of whatever happens. You have a very clear and grounded perspective on things and you're happy to put time and energy into the areas of your life that aren't running as smoothly as you'd like. You'll also put a lot of elbow grease into all physical activities, especially if there's a competitive element involved.

• *Thursday 6 September* •

If your confidence suffers a knock today, try not to take it too much to heart. Perhaps someone in authority is testing you in some way and you may suddenly get an attack of nerves or be plagued by a moment's self-doubt. Above all, don't be too hard on yourself or lose sight of the fact that you're more than capable of taking on this challenge.

• *Friday 7 September* •

Yesterday's trials and tribulations are well behind you and your mood is much more outgoing and self-assured today. You're also feeling very sociable, so it's a wonderful time for a reunion with some favourite friends. A close personal relationship will benefit enormously from your input, as you'll be able to draw from your experience and instinctively know what to say, especially if it concerns matters of the heart.

• *Saturday 8 September* •

It's one of those days when you're itching to get to the shops and part with some of your hard-earned cash. You're in the mood to pamper yourself, which means that you'll probably end up spending more than you intended. But you're more likely to come to the conclusion that life is too short to worry about that sort of thing than to give yourself any grief over spoiling yourself.

• *Sunday 9 September* •

Although today is traditionally a day of rest, you're in no mood to take it easy. You're full of dynamic energy and you want to roll up your sleeves and get stuck into some hard work. If anything around the house needs a total overhaul, you'll take great pleasure in repairing it and restoring it to its original condition. You'll also be able to tackle any financial matters with equal gusto. Wow!

• *Monday 10 September* •

You are scratching your head today trying to puzzle out a certain person's behaviour. Whether you can fathom them out or not, it will definitely serve as a reminder of the depth and complexity of human nature. You'll be drawn to people and situations that make you question the way you look at things, and a fascinating discussion with a friend or colleague could give you a whole new insight into yourself.

• *Tuesday 11 September* •

Your mind is very clear and concise today. If you are going to an interview or talking to an important client or authority figure, you're bound to make a very favourable impression. You're also at your most inspired and able to combine analytical reasoning with creatively inspired thinking. This winning formula will stand you in excellent stead professionally, as well as making you feel more complete in yourself.

• *Wednesday 12 September* •

Your intuition is heightened today and you're very aware of the thoughts and feelings of the people around you. You're able to empathize with others and listen to someone who needs to talk, yet you won't get bogged down in their problems. You're also feeling very motivated so you'll want to put some of your skills and strengths to good use.

• *Thursday 13 September* •

This is another great day to show off your talents, because others will be very responsive to your bright ideas. You're ready to set the ball rolling and start a new project, and you have the drive and inspiration to set the wheels in motion. Not only that, you'll also be able to count on the support of people who believe in you and your abilities. Someone could pay you a compliment that will have you walking on air. How nice!

• *Friday 14 September* •

Listen to your intuition today because it will tell you how to negotiate a business deal or handle some kind of important discussion. Although these ideas may come out of the blue, they'll make perfect sense and you'll probably wonder why you hadn't thought of them before. You could also get a surprise phone call or letter from someone you have mixed feelings about. Do you really still want them in your life?

• *Saturday 15 September* •

You'll be very pleased with the progress you make on the home front today, especially if you're prepared to roll up your sleeves and tackle the really boring but necessary jobs. This could involve sorting through those piles of clutter you've accumulated and throwing out what's no longer needed, or doing a thorough clean in the places that normally get neglected. Dusters to the ready!

• *Sunday 16 September* •

If you managed to do a lot of clearing out yesterday you might feel rather depleted today. This could be more on the emotional than the physical level, especially if you found papers or photographs from the past that struck a deep chord. Maybe some old memories were stirred up. If so, allow yourself some time to remember before you get back to your busy life.

• *Monday 17 September* •

You're feeling very close to your family today and you'll want to spend as much time with them as possible. The New Moon is opening you up emotionally to your nearest and dearest, so this is a good time to talk about any issues that you may not have felt able to discuss before. Although this may bring up some painful emotions, it will also strengthen the bond between you.

• *Tuesday 18 September* •

If you're currently between relationships, keep a lookout today because you could come across someone who really grabs your interest. At first you may feel as if it's simply a meeting of minds and that the attraction goes no deeper than that, but you might then begin to notice that you can't get them out of your thoughts. Watch this space!

• *Wednesday 19 September* •

This is a good day to sign any agreements or enter into a negotiation of some kind. You have a good working relationship with others and you can come to a mutually beneficial arrangement. You can also explain exactly where you stand on some very important issues, leaving no room for doubt or misunderstandings. With everything so straightforward and clear-cut, you can confidently anticipate a successful outcome.

• *Thursday 20 September* •

It's a marvellous day for taking part in a discussion or debate because you're very confident about your beliefs and quite happy to speak your mind. Don't be surprised if you're praised for the articulate way in which you express yourself. You might even acquire a few admirers who are charmed by your eloquence. You're also in the mood for a bit of fun, so get together with some friends if possible.

• *Friday 21 September* •

Think about what you would ideally like to do today and then get going. You can achieve more than you realize simply by adopting a positive and methodical approach. You'll thoroughly enjoy channelling your energies into whatever you really want to do, and you can confidently assume that you'll meet any deadlines that you've set for yourself. Talk about efficient!

• *Saturday 22 September* •

Family life takes priority today and you'll want to get together with relatives to do some socializing. Perhaps there's a reunion of some kind that you're all going to, giving you the chance to meet up with people you haven't seen for a while. You could form a stronger bond with a family member who hasn't been the easiest person to get on with recently, but is now ready to let bygones be bygones.

• *Sunday 23 September* •

It is really easy to speak from the heart today and express exactly how you're feeling. This bodes well for any kind of romantic relationship you're involved in, especially as your other half is likely to reciprocate and share with you the strength of their feelings. It's also a great day for enjoying a favourite hobby or pastime because you're at your most creative and inspired.

• *Monday 24 September* •

You'll really feel the benefits today of any improvements you have made to the most important areas of your life. Relationships in particular are beginning to change for the better and you're feeling a lot more aware of what makes you happy and fulfilled. There could also be some good news connected to a joint money matter, making you feel distinctly better off.

• *Tuesday 25 September* •

It's another enjoyable day when you can revel in the company of friends and family. You could receive an invitation to go and stay with someone that you don't see a great deal of, or you may decide to have a few people over for a meal and a good old natter. You'll get far more pleasure from giving than receiving, and you'll be only too happy to thoroughly spoil your loved ones.

• *Wednesday 26 September* •

You have the Midas touch today and everything you do will turn out favourably. You feel positive and full of optimism, and your intuition is telling you that it's one of those lucky days when you're able to go with the flow and know that life will provide you with everything you need. Not that you intend to sit back and wait for things to happen – you'll be leading from the front and loving every minute of it!

• *Thursday 27 September* •

You're able to work to a schedule today without getting bored or distracted. You'll give your best performance if you have total autonomy and you don't have to answer to anyone else. Not only will this allow you to be more your own person, it will also give you the opportunity to show others how disciplined and motivated you are.

• *Friday 28 September* •

Someone who holds you in very high esteem gives your morale a boost today. This could be a fellow professional who admires your work, or a loved one who wants you to know how special they think you are. If you've been wondering where a particular relationship is going, what transpires in the coming days will remove any doubts that you had.

• *Saturday 29 September* •

You're in the mood to step back from your everyday life and do something with mystical or spiritual overtones. You're also feeling very selfless and compassionate, making you want to do something for the benefit of others. Offering your services will feel very uplifting and worthwhile, especially if it involves those who are less fortunate than yourself. If a loved one is in need of some care and attention, don't forget that charity begins at home.

• *Sunday 30 September* •

Getting on with other people is as easy as ABC but a lot more enjoyable today! You'll especially like spending time alone with someone special and keeping the rest of the world at bay. If you are out and about socializing, you'll prefer to have an in-depth conversation with one person rather than chat to lots of different people about nothing in particular.

OCTOBER AT A GLANCE

Love	♥ ♥ ♥ ♥ ♥
Money	£ $
Career	💻 💻 💻 💻 💻
Health	☼ ☼ ☼ ☼ ☼

• *Monday 1 October* •

Actions definitely speak louder than words right now and you'll want to show a certain someone how deeply committed you are to them. Perhaps you could buy them a gift that you know they'll really appreciate and which will in some way seal the bond of affection between you. If you've recently started a relationship with someone, it looks as if it will be everything you expect it to be today – and more!

• *Tuesday 2 October* •

The winds of change blow from an unexpected direction today, catching you off guard. This trend is likely to continue for the next couple of weeks, with plans and schedules being disrupted and changed at the last minute. Fortunately, today's unforeseen events won't throw you into too much of a spin and you'll soon get back on top of things. Write down any brainwaves, otherwise they could be gone with the wind!

• *Wednesday 3 October* •

You feel happy and contented today. People can't help but notice your inner glow. You feel very open and loving towards everyone and you could strike up an instant friendship with someone new that you meet. Make the most of this wonderfully sociable mood and get together with some of your favourite people. A cultural activity could be fun.

• *Thursday 4 October* •

You can cover a lot of ground today and achieve a tremendous amount. You'll inspire everyone around you with your incredible energy and dedication, and if you're in a position of authority you'll be able to introduce some new ideas without being challenged on them. A younger person will look to you for guidance or assistance, and you'll draw on your experience and knowledge to help them.

• *Friday 5 October* •

You instinctively feel like withdrawing today and giving yourself some time to mull things over. You've been very productive and resourceful recently and you might still have some plans in the pipeline that you want to think about. Alternatively you could bounce your ideas off a trusted friend and see what suggestions they come up with. You know what they say about two heads being better than one.

• *Saturday 6 October* •

You want to keep busy today and not sit around taking life easy. However, make sure that you're being productive for a purpose. If you start slowing down at the end of the day, focus your attention on more leisurely pursuits like reading a good book or doing some cooking. Your mind will carry on being active even if you physically peter out.

• *Sunday 7 October* •

Relationships run smoothly today and you'll feel in particular harmony with a certain person. Simply being in each other's company will enhance your sense of well-being and make you feel more alert. Your powers of concentration are ace at the moment and you'll be able to put your mind to almost anything. And if you're a typical Gemini, that's exactly what you will do!

• *Monday 8 October* •

If a problem hanging over you has been creating a lot of stress and tension, you'll come up with a brilliant solution to resolve it today. It will be so simple that you'll want to kick yourself for not thinking of it before. Don't be too hard on yourself, however, because you probably needed to give yourself some time to come up with a creative way of dealing with the matter.

• *Tuesday 9 October* •

You can move mountains today and that's exactly what you will do. You're in a very ambitious and expansive mood, and are determined to put yourself to the fore. Luck is also on your side and you could be presented with an unexpected opportunity to shine. Not that you'll leave anything to chance. Whatever falls in your lap will be backed up with a confident and assertive move on your part. You are unstoppable!

• *Wednesday 10 October* •

You'll invest a lot of energy in your finances today, and the more thoughtful and focused you are the better the results will be. It's an excellent time to discuss any joint financial arrangements, especially if one of you has a more liberal approach to spending than the other. Working as a team and seeing how you can make the most of your resources is your best approach, although it may take a little while for this to happen.

• *Thursday 11 October* •

You're in full command of yourself today and you're all set to make a dazzling impression. This is the time to act boldly and to seize every opportunity to fulfil your heart's desire. Knowing what you want and knowing how to go about getting it gives you a wonderful feeling of power, and others will be amazed by your resolution and determination. Could they also be slightly envious?

• Friday 12 October •

You're on top form again today and you can make just about anything happen through the sheer force of your willpower. You'll know exactly where and how to use your energy for maximum effect and minimum stress. You're also in the perfect position to call the shots where a business partner or associate is concerned, and you'll have a positive influence on any discussions that take place. What a fantastic day!

• Saturday 13 October •

You're a real live wire today and you'll want to pack as much excitement and variety into your day as possible. Ideally, you'd like to be on the move and have lots of changes of scene. If you live in a town, you might feel like getting out into the countryside and having a long walk. On the other hand, if you live in a rural area you'll like nothing more than being in the hustle and bustle of an urban landscape. After all, variety is the spice of life.

• Sunday 14 October •

A potentially sticky situation between you and a loved one needs careful handling today. One of you may be spoiling for a fight, so the atmosphere between you will be very combustible. If you are the one who is feeling tetchy, work off your mood by doing something physical. If you are the one who is about to get it in the neck, try not to rise to the bait as that will only inflame the situation.

• *Monday 15 October* •

Good news if you are currently single! Matters of the heart take a turn for the better today, and between now and the middle of November you will be at your most magnetic. Accept all invitations that come your way, even if some of them don't look like the sort of thing you normally go to. It might just be that you're destined to meet your next partner at one of those occasions.

• *Tuesday 16 October* •

Your social life is really perking up and you can expect to be in demand over the coming weeks. Ideally, you'll want to spend today with people that you really care about and do something that everyone will enjoy. You're in a very demonstrative and affectionate mood, and you'll want to show your loved ones how much you appreciate them. You're also bound to receive a few compliments yourself. What a wonderful day to look forward to!

• *Wednesday 17 October* •

Your mind is very alert today and you could easily go into overdrive if you're not careful. You've got a lot to think about as well as a lot to process, so you need to give yourself time to get to grips with everything. Do yourself a favour and don't take on any more than you can handle right now. It could make the difference between staying on top of things and getting snowed under.

• *Thursday 18 October* •

If you still have a lot on your plate today and things don't look like easing up, you may find you need to delegate simply to keep ahead. Your energy may start to flag and you'll need to find some way of recharging your batteries. It's a very good day for exploring techniques connected with mind over matter, such as visualizing yourself in a calm and relaxed state. Meditation or yoga might help.

• *Friday 19 October* •

You need to be rather circumspect today where finances are concerned and resist any temptation you might have to play fast and loose. It's not a good day to commit to anything in writing, and even verbal agreements are best avoided. Your best course of action is probably to do nothing and put things on hold for the time being. Be particularly wary of someone who seems to promise the earth but who is really full of hot air.

• *Saturday 20 October* •

You feel very connected to a loved one today and you'll be so identified with each other's feelings that it will be hard to know where you end and they start. You'll want to enjoy this state of bliss without any interruptions from the outside world, so try to get as much privacy as possible. If you're currently unattached, a certain someone is about to be mesmerized by your seductive charms. How romantic!

• *Sunday 21 October* •

Life promises both contentment and stability today, and you'll be quite happy to while away the time in enjoyable conversation with your nearest and dearest. If you have anything important to discuss, you'll find it easy to say what you mean without causing any offence or upset. Quite the opposite, in fact – others are likely to treat your ideas and opinions with respect and give you a full vote of confidence.

• *Monday 22 October* •

It may be Monday but you certainly won't have the blues. Your diary is bursting with interesting dates and appointments and there are plenty of people you want to see. It's a day for enjoying yourself, so you won't want to get bogged down with anything dreary or routine. If that means doing something that will make your working day more interesting, don't waste a moment in making that a reality.

• Tuesday 23 October •

You're raring to go and anything that's been held up recently will suddenly start to move again. This may mean that you'll be rushed off your feet but you'll thrive on all the activity that's around you and the adrenalin alone will keep you going for as long as necessary. Action is your middle name at the moment and the current pace of life suits you just fine.

• Wednesday 24 October •

You're in a rather outspoken mood and you might need to curb your tongue lest you come out with something that's a little too close to the bone. Your insights are dazzlingly perceptive but, although you may not intend them to be hurtful in any way, the person on the receiving end may not feel the same way. If you honestly feel you should say what you think, try to find a more subtle approach.

• Thursday 25 October •

You can enjoy a day of relative calm and use the time to take stock of recent events. You've been so caught up with the present that you may not have had time to think about the future and where you see yourself going. You can achieve great things now if you put your mind to it, so draw up a plan and decide on a strategy to get you from A to B. It's that simple.

• Friday 26 October •

You're very sure of yourself where it comes to finances and work, and you may get the chance today to show the world how capable and resourceful you are. You'll act from a position of strength if you have to discuss or negotiate anything, and you'll know exactly what you should say and do. You might be so effective that you are offered a bigger and better package than you expected.

• *Saturday 27 October* •

The very constructive advice that you offer someone today will consolidate your relationship with them in some way. Perhaps the interest you show and the time you invest in helping them will reassure them that they can trust you, especially if they tend to be rather wary. You won't want to wander far afield this weekend, so arrange to do some nice things at home.

• *Sunday 28 October* •

You're full of brilliant ideas for making changes to your home today, and you'll want to rope in as many people as possible to help you put them into action. Maybe you've decided that you need more living space, so you want to move some of the furniture around. Fortunately, everyone will agree with you, and you'll be able to make this a family project. Have fun!

• *Monday 29 October* •

A whole new aspect of your personality is now emerging and you may feel as if you're shedding an old skin. You feel tremendously energetic and motivated, and you're in no doubt about who you are and how you want to live your life. Although you may not fancy taking a long hard look at the past, it may be time to think about letting go of anything that doesn't belong to your future.

• *Tuesday 30 October* •

Think about your general well-being today and decide if there's anything you need to improve or change. Maybe you need to kick a habit that's interfering with your health and preventing you from feeling at your best. If you feel you could do with a general check-up, organize it now while it's uppermost in your mind.

• Wednesday 31 October •

Floating on Cloud Nine? You're in love with love today and you might be inspired to find a creative or artistic outlet for your feelings. For instance, you might feel like writing a poem or doing some painting, or you may simply want to listen to some romantic music and think about you-know-who. If you decide to declare yourself, you'll find the perfect words to communicate what's in your heart.

NOVEMBER AT A GLANCE

Love	♥ ♥ ♥ ♥ ♥
Money	£ $
Career	💻 💻 💻 💻 💻
Health	☼ ☼ ☼ ☼ ☼

• Thursday 1 November •

Be careful not to fall into any rigid thinking patterns today as you may not be able to see the woods for the trees. The problem is that you're so focused on seeing things in one particular way that you block out the rest of the picture. The Full Moon is intensifying your vision, but it's in danger of becoming tunnel vision unless you make a conscious effort to keep an open mind.

• Friday 2 November •

You're feeling very bright and breezy today, and quite happy to go with the flow. You're also full of gratitude because someone who believes in you sings your praises and puts in a good word for you to the powers-that-be. What's more, someone who's been admiring you from a distance suddenly decides to show you how much they think of you. Aren't you popular!

• *Saturday 3 November* •

Set aside some time for yourself today as you'll want to ponder over recent developments. Some sober reflection is probably needed about a certain person. Perhaps you feel that they have overstepped the mark in some way and you now no longer know where you stand with them. Try to get out into the fresh air at some point and blow away any cobwebs.

• *Sunday 4 November* •

If you fancy a change of scene today, why not do something different that will lighten your mood and give you something interesting to think about? This is a very good way to recharge your batteries, especially if you can spend the day with a kindred spirit and have a really good chat. If you want to get something off your chest, this is the perfect time to do so.

• *Monday 5 November* •

Good fortune is on your side today and you'll have the chance to carve a new professional niche for yourself. Many doors will now begin to open for you and you'll be given the opportunity to show how serious and committed you are to realizing your goals. A woman may help you to consolidate your position, perhaps through an introduction or a word in someone's ear. You're on the up and up!

• *Tuesday 6 November* •

You're in the mood to let your hair down today and be with people that you feel completely at home with. You'll especially enjoy getting together with close family members and reminiscing about the past. If anyone else is feeling senti-mental, you'll love nothing more than taking a walk down memory lane together and remembering times gone by. Shar-ing a delicious meal and making a real occasion of it would be a wonderful way to create some new memories.

• *Wednesday 7 November* •

You feel very enthusiastic today and you can't wait to put some of your good ideas into practice. You're so keen to make things happen that you could get carried away and overlook some important details. By all means keep your focus on the bigger picture, but you won't get anything off the ground unless you make sure that the nuts and bolts are in place. Unfortunately, it's a case of 99 per cent perspiration and 1 per cent inspiration.

• *Thursday 8 November* •

Today finds you feeling much more conscientious, and you'll be more than willing to put in some extra hours in order to get ahead with what you're doing. The next fortnight looks like being one of the hardest working and most productive periods of the year, and one in which you'll be determined to achieve your very best. You're at your most industrious and inspired, and nothing and no one can hold you back from your chosen path.

• *Friday 9 November* •

You will feel very encouraged by today's events and you'll be given every indication that the efforts you're currently making will soon start to pay off. You could also hear some good news on the health front, which will come as a huge relief. If you've been thinking about getting a pet but can't quite decide what you would like, sauntering past the pet shop could make your mind up for you.

• *Saturday 10 November* •

It will do you the world of good to stay at home today and put your feet up for a few hours. With the hectic pace of life that you're currently experiencing, there probably hasn't been a lot of time for your close relationships recently. Make a conscious decision to spend time with you-know-who and enjoy each other's company. Even simple pleasures will feel wonderfully gratifying and comforting now.

• *Sunday 11 November* •

Someone you thought you could count on proves to be more elusive than you imagined, and you can't help feeling disappointed. Try to take it in your stride and decide whether it was your unrealistic expectations that let you down rather than the other person. It looks as though someone else is determined to do whatever will needle you. How irritating!

• *Monday 12 November* •

If you're annoyed by the way someone behaved yesterday, be prepared to have a frank discussion with them today and say exactly what you think. You'll be surprised at how receptive they are to your comments, as long as you don't overdo it and make them feel as if they've committed a cardinal sin. A colleague or boss could expect you to have all the answers to a particular problem and you'll have to do some quick thinking. Easy for a Gemini like you!

• *Tuesday 13 November* •

What's the matter? You're feeling overly sensitive today and liable to take offence where none is intended. Perhaps a certain someone inadvertently touches a raw nerve and is taken aback by the intensity of your reaction. This may be an ideal opportunity to realize that you're still feeling hurt about something and that it may be time to let it go, especially if it's adversely affecting your current relationships.

• *Wednesday 14 November* •

Be careful that you don't overreach yourself today and bite off more than you can chew. You may have an exaggerated belief in what you're capable of at the moment, and unless you take a more realistic attitude to things, you could let yourself and others down. That isn't to say that you should curb your ambition entirely, but it does mean that you should bear in mind your limitations.

• *Thursday 15 November* •

Brace yourself today for a much-needed re-evaluation of your working practices and the relationship you have with colleagues. Today's New Moon is urging you to confront the fact that if someone isn't pulling their weight, it's now time to tell them how angry and resentful you feel about it. If you're to work together in a productive way, you can no longer afford to carry any passengers. If they don't shape up, they'll have to ship out.

• *Friday 16 November* •

It's not an easy day for partnerships and if you get involved in any discussions or arguments they are likely to end on rather a sour note. That's because no one is prepared to back down and admit they're wrong, let alone concede that the other person has a point. You may need to spend some time apart until you're ready to work at resolving your differences. Try not to make it more of a problem than it really is.

• *Saturday 17 November* •

This could be another day of embattled egos, with each person fighting hard to stand their ground. Having the courage of your convictions may be very important to you right now, and giving way on something you passionately believe in won't wash with you in the slightest. However, forcing your ideas on other people will only serve to alienate them, and that may be a heavy price to pay.

• *Sunday 18 November* •

You're feeling very inspired today and you can trust your hunches because they're unerringly accurate. This will pay dividends in every area of your life, but particularly where you need to clear up any recent misunderstandings. Set aside some time to be at home with your loved ones and initiate an open discussion about any grievances anyone may have. Talking things through will enable everyone to forgive and forget.

• *Monday 19 November* •

Adopt a cool, rational approach to solve a work-related difficulty today. It's important that you get to the root of the problem without becoming emotionally heated, as that will only confuse the situation. Provided you keep a level head, you'll soon be able to clarify the situation and find a way forward. If you're feeling under the weather, it might be time for a tonic to boost your immune system.

• *Tuesday 20 November* •

You feel like a psychic sponge today and it will be hard to separate your feelings from those of everyone around you. If you're subject to strange mood shifts and wonder why you're feeling this way, you may be absorbing the emotional state of someone close to you. Your interest in the mysteries of life will be stimulated, especially if you have a telepathic link with a certain person.

• *Wednesday 21 November* •

Set your sights high today and don't allow a fear of failure to hold you back. You have everything to play for and it would be a shame to restrict your thinking at a time when the sky really is the limit. Don't make the mistake either of talking to someone who might dismiss out of hand something you're excited about. Believe in yourself and you won't go far wrong.

• *Thursday 22 November* •

An exciting day is in store for you, especially if you have a romantic date all lined up. You're feeling very amorous and sensual, and in the mood for an intimate encounter. If you meet someone today and there's a strong physical attraction between you, don't necessarily expect a long-term relationship to come out of it. That's not to say that you won't have fun while it lasts!

• *Friday 23 November* •

Your thoughts turn to the festivities ahead today and you might decide to buy a few early Christmas presents for your nearest and dearest. You may have a sudden burst of inspiration and know exactly what you want to get for certain people. You'll also be prepared to give someone the benefit of the doubt and put a recent upset behind you.

• *Saturday 24 November* •

You're probably still catching your breath after yesterday's burst of activity. In fact, you're quite happy to have a low-key day and not do anything too demanding or ambitious. You could run into difficulties if a loved one wants you to be more involved with their plans for the day. With luck, they'll be willing to indulge you, provided you manage to reassure them that they're still the most important thing in the world to you.

• *Sunday 25 November* •

If you still feel like doing your own thing today, you'll be able to get your way without coming on too strong. Your charm alone will give you a lot of mileage, coupled with the fact that a certain someone will no doubt realize that it makes a lot more sense to let you get on with whatever you feel you must do. Being true to yourself is vital now, and who can argue with that?

• *Monday 26 November* •

It doesn't matter how hard you try to make headway today – you'll end up feeling as if the brakes are on. Perhaps you come up against a rule or regulation that you can't get past, despite thinking up some very creative solutions. If there's no way round it, you'll need to redirect your energies and find a challenge that you can succeed in.

• *Tuesday 27 November* •

Switch your focus today onto how you can introduce your broader vision into your daily life. You can act now with great courage and confidence, installing new beliefs into an old and outworn system. You could even act as a pioneer and wake people up to a more innovative way of doing things. If you dare to be different, you'll be surprised by how quickly everyone else will catch up with you.

• *Wednesday 28 November* •

If a financial matter has run into difficulty recently, this is a very good day for sorting things out. It may take some working out, but you have the energy and determination to put things right. Your serious and responsible approach will inspire trust and respect from the powers-that-be, and if you need to ask for a loan of some kind they'll be favourably disposed towards you. That's a relief!

• *Thursday 29 November* •

You're in a very dreamy and reflective mood today and you'll be looking at the world through very rosy glasses. You want to see the best in everyone and you won't want to get involved in any dramas or challenging situations. You're also not in the mood to make any commitments, and you'll be much happier mulling over any ideas or projects for a while before you say yes.

• *Friday 30 November* •

Today's Full Moon presents you with a moral dilemma of some kind over the next two weeks. Your code of ethics will be tested, and you will have to give very serious consideration to how you should respond to a certain proposition. Although you might normally want to be very honest in a situation like this, the intensity of your emotions could cloud your judgment now. Talk things through with a trusted friend before you go any further.

DECEMBER AT A GLANCE

Love	♥ ♥ ♥ ♥ ♥
Money	£
Career	💻 💻 💻 💻 💻
Health	☼ ☼ ☼ ☼

• *Saturday 1 December* •

Try to be as open as possible today and don't hold back from expressing what's really on your mind. Your other half will really appreciate you sharing your feelings with them, especially if something has remained unspoken between you for a while. They'll also be extremely relieved that you have enough trust and confidence in them to reveal your innermost thoughts.

• *Sunday 2 December* •

Home comforts mean a lot to you today and you'll feel most comfortable spending time at home with your nearest and dearest. If a family member has been having a bad time recently, you may be called upon to offer some moral support. You're also in the mood for being productive and doing something worthwhile, and you might decide to do some odd jobs around the house.

• *Monday 3 December* •

How are your plans for Christmas coming along? You're full of ambitious plans today and you'll throw yourself into organizing whatever you will be doing over the festive season. Remember to pace yourself, though, otherwise you'll expend all your energy in the preparations and have none left on the actual day. If someone is less than enthusiastic about some of your ideas, give them a wide berth until they cheer up a bit.

• *Tuesday 4 December* •

Although you want to be open to a certain person's suggestion, you can't help being sceptical about their motives. For some reason they lack credibility in your eyes, so you're reluctant to go along with anything they're saying. Let them know that you've got your doubts and that you need more time to think things over. If they're worth their salt, they'll respect your wishes.

• *Wednesday 5 December* •

You'll have no difficulty voicing your feelings and emotions today, and you'll want to show a loved one how wonderful you think they are. A love affair could turn a corner, and you might come up with a very romantic way of saying in both word and deed what the relationship means to you. By the same token, someone who feels passionately about you could be about to make a very big proposal. Got any clues who this is?

• *Thursday 6 December* •

Even though your hunches are fairly reliable today, don't trust to luck too much because there's a chance that not everything will turn out the way you'd like. If you're intending to take a calculated risk of some kind, make sure that you really do calculate the odds of pulling it off before you go sailing into the unknown. A deep and thought-provoking conversation with a loved one could provide you with some very valuable insights into your relationship.

• *Friday 7 December* •

You're in a very organized and businesslike mood today, and you'll get things done in a brisk and efficient manner. You're on solid ground and confident about what you're doing, which means you'll be able to make a great deal of progress. You'll also be quite happy to work overtime and get the job done, even if that means forgoing a social arrangement. Never mind, there'll be no shortage of those in the coming weeks.

• *Saturday 8 December* •

You feel extremely positive today and no challenge will be too daunting for you. Whether you're elbowing your way through the Christmas shoppers or giving the house a thorough once over before the festivities, your energy will ensure that you achieve everything you set out to do. Watch any over-zealous tendencies on your part where a family member is concerned, as they could feel you're trying to control them.

• *Sunday 9 December* •

You can share some wonderful moments of closeness with a relative today, which will be beneficial both physically and emotionally. You feel so in tune with this person that much of your communication will be unspoken. You could also feel very inspired to think about some New Year resolutions, especially if they involve forging closer relationships with the people you love.

• *Monday 10 December* •

Someone starts to have a very powerful effect on you, and you'll find it hard to get them out of your thoughts. If you don't know this person already, you could easily come across them while you're out and about today. They could be connected to your work in some way, so if you've got an appointment with someone you haven't met before, brace yourself for quite an impact!

• *Tuesday 11 December* •

A loved one seems determined to annoy you today and it'll be hard not to lose your cool and bite back at them. Just why they seem so intent on giving you a hard time is not clear, but you're really not in the mood to put up with such behaviour. Do your best to find out what's at the root of their irritability, but if they won't let you near them, your best bet is to let them stew.

• *Wednesday 12 December* •

Someone might impose their will on you today, making you feel as if you're being backed into a corner. You won't react well to such forceful tactics being used on you, and you'll have no hesitation in showing this person that you don't take kindly to being pushed around. If you're interested in sussing out why they're so determined to do things their way, you must first get past their defence mechanisms. Easier said than done!

• *Thursday 13 December* •

It's a great day for being sociable as you're on sparkling form. It's the party season and your head is probably in a spin from all the invitations to choose from. You'll really enjoy doing anything at the last minute, especially if there's a chance to meet some new people. You have no desire to spend time with the same old crowd, and the more you can move out of your normal social sphere the happier you'll be. Have fun!

• *Friday 14 December* •

You could hear something today that produces a strong emotional reaction in you. Powerful feelings of jealousy or possessiveness could threaten to engulf you, making you react without thinking. Alternatively, a certain someone might overpower you with the intensity of their feelings for you, making you feel rather uncomfortable. Perhaps that is because you are unable to reciprocate, in which case you may have to be cruel to be kind.

• *Saturday 15 December* •

You're in the mood to do some spending today and splash out on Christmas presents for your nearest and dearest. If you come across something that you really like, you may even decide to treat yourself as well. Because you're in such a gregarious and outgoing frame of mind, you might decide to invite a friend along and make it a fun day out. The more the merrier!

• *Sunday 16 December* •

If you're counting the cost of yesterday's outing and feeling out of pocket, you may well be thinking about ways to increase your income today. You won't even have to think very hard because ideas will seemingly come out of nowhere. If you bounce some of these off a partner or colleague, together you can come up with a scheme that will be a real money-spinner.

• *Monday 17 December* •

There is a lot to do today and you could end up feeling under pressure to get everything done. Don't be tempted, however, to take any shortcuts because you'll almost inevitably have to go back to square one again. Try to adopt a methodical approach to your workload, and recognize that there are only so many hours in the day. What doesn't get done today will just have to wait until tomorrow.

• *Tuesday 18 December* •

Work is probably the last place you want to be today and you'll find it hard to sustain your interest in anything mundane or routine. Fortunately the Christmas spirit is creating a light-hearted and festive mood, and no one will be much in the mood to toil away. There might even be a get-together at some point, which will please the party animal in you no end.

• *Wednesday 19 December* •

Your social life is in full swing now and you're determined to make the most of this fabulous time. There's a wonderfully bright and festive atmosphere, helping you to get on well with whoever you meet. It's a fantastic day for going out with a group of friends or colleagues and having a slap-up meal somewhere really fun.

• *Thursday 20 December* •

Your head is in the clouds today and, if you have nothing better to do, you'll quite happily while away the time day-dreaming. If you have important tasks on the agenda, it could be a struggle to keep your mind on what you are doing. Maybe the answer is to give yourself frequent breaks while working on anything routine. However, you will be inspired when it comes to using your imagination.

• *Friday 21 December* •

If you're a typical Gemini, you'll be happy to let your mind wander off into all sorts of new directions today. You feel tremendously inspired and you're already thinking ahead to the New Year and all the plans and ideas you want to put into practice. If you fancy branching out into a different field, start drawing up a list of requirements that are important to you. Set your sights high and you'll achieve more than you thought possible.

• *Saturday 22 December* •

Pace yourself as much as possible today because you could easily feel worn out if you continue to go hell for leather. It seems as if all and sundry are making demands on you, and even if you would like to please them it will be physically impossible to do everything that's expected of you. Don't be afraid to say no, and give yourself a break if you're flagging. After all, you want to be your best for next week's festivities, don't you?

• *Sunday 23 December* •

It's a wonderful day to have a heart-to-heart with a partner and talk about how you feel. You'll find it very easy to relate to each other, and you'll discover that you have a lot more in common than you realized. Perhaps you're ready to drop your guard and reveal a much deeper and more private side of your personality that you haven't wanted to expose before. You'll also be very willing to listen, and this will bring you both a lot closer.

• *Monday 24 December* •

Fun is your middle name today and you'll want to enjoy the company of as many friends and family as you can. You're in very high spirits and just being in your company will make others feel as if they've been sprinkled with fairy dust. The Christmas celebrations promise to go with a swing and if guests are staying with you you'll all get on like a house on fire. What a magical day!

• *Tuesday 25 December* •

Happy Christmas! Get set for a hugely enjoyable day with everyone on good form and delighted to be together. You're feeling very loving towards everyone, and the more people who join you the happier you'll feel. You're in quite an indulgent mood and you won't want to restrain yourself where food and drink are concerned. Live now, pay later is definitely your motto for the day. Have a great time!

• *Wednesday 26 December* •

You want to take today at a nice, leisurely pace and enjoy some peace and quiet. You might feel like taking a relaxing walk with some family members so you can get some fresh air. If you're invited out anywhere, you'll be happiest in an intimate gathering and you'll love nothing more than having a cosy *tête-à-tête* with someone that you can completely relax with.

• *Thursday 27 December* •

Your love life will bring you plenty of joy and happiness today, and you'll really appreciate a gesture on the part of your loved one. Perhaps they're in a particularly demonstrative mood, and the tender loving care they show you leaves you in no doubt of how valued and appreciated you are. If you're concerned about someone's welfare, try to help them over the next day or so if you can.

• *Friday 28 December* •

You're beginning to gear yourself up for the end of year celebrations today and you'll be busy making last-minute arrangements. If you're rested and fully recovered from the excesses of this week, you'll be quite happy to let yourself be swept along by the social current that seems to be picking up momentum again. The next few days could bring a few surprises on the social front so keep your arrangements flexible.

• *Saturday 29 December* •

You're full of bright ideas today on how to keep everyone in good spirits and sustain the festive atmosphere. You'll rise to the occasion if you're doing any entertaining, and your ready wit and engaging conversation will make you the centre of attention. You're also in the mood for a few practical jokes, but try not to let your sense of humour get too out of hand. Not everyone is as game for a laugh as you!

• *Sunday 30 December* •

Someone is being very inflexible today and they'll refuse to budge on a certain issue. Not only will this test your patience to the limit, it will also make you question why this person is in your life. Perhaps you've spent more time with them over these last few days than normal, and it's revealed various aspects of their character that you really don't like. If you challenge them on their behaviour, expect some kind of showdown.

• *Monday 31 December* •

It's more than likely that you'll be here, there and everywhere today as you won't be able to turn down a single invitation. Although you'll really enjoy being with friends and loved ones in comfortable and familiar surroundings for part of the time, your curious Gemini spirit won't be able to resist going out and meeting new people as well. Sounds like you're going to have a whale of a time!

YOUR GEMINI SUN SIGN

In this chapter I am going to tell you all about your Sun sign. But what is a Sun sign? It often gets called a star sign, but are they the same thing? Well, yes, although 'Sun sign' is a more accurate term. Your Sun sign is the sign that the Sun occupied when you were born. Every year, the Sun moves through the heavens and spends an average of 30 days in each of the twelve signs. When you were born, the Sun was moving through the sign of Gemini, so this is your Sun or star sign.

This chapter tells you everything you want to know about your Sun sign. To start off, I describe your general personality – what makes you tick. Then I talk about your attitude to relationships, the way you handle money, what your Sun sign says about your health and, finally, which careers are best for you. Put all that together and you will have a well-rounded picture of yourself.

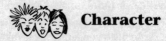 **Character**

Gemini is one of the most lively and vibrant signs of the zodiac. You are mercurial, bright and terrific company. Even better, you don't seem to age, and even when you're older than you care to remember you will still look years younger. Your attitude will also be a lot more youthful than your contemporaries. You love keeping up with the latest trends and your insatiable curiosity makes you as interested in knowing what your best friend is doing as what's happening on the other side of the world. The growth of the Internet and the entire technological revolution is a real gift for you because it has opened up whole new areas of communication to explore. Not only can you continue to enjoy reading books, magazines and newspapers, you can now chat to complete strangers through the ether and order your groceries through the television. And as for mobile phones, well, a chatterbox like you is in heaven!

It's certainly important for you to keep in touch with people, and if you are on the Internet you probably e-mail friends and family in the four corners of the globe. But you are just as happy chatting to your next-door neighbour or getting together with friends. And if you are in the right mood you will gladly strike up a conversation with the person standing behind you in the supermarket queue or sitting next to you on the bus. Is this a polite way of saying you love gossiping? Well, yes, actually. There's nothing you like better than being first with the news – 'Remember, you heard it here first,' you'll say as you impart the latest snippet of information.

It's all thanks to your ruler, Mercury. He rules communications and so makes you very eloquent. You're a born communicator and find it easy to express your ideas. Mercury is a liquid metal and you also like to keep things fluid. In fact, you can be really restless at times, unable to settle down to anything for long. As a result, you have a low boredom threshold and can find it difficult to concentrate on one thing for very long unless you're absolutely enraptured by it. If you're not careful, this can lead to a superficial approach, with lots of projects left unfinished.

Versatility is your middle name and you can tackle most things. You're also very adaptable, although sometimes this turns into moodiness and inconsistency. You believe that you operate on a steady, even keel but the people in your life might not agree. Yes, your emotions take dramatic dips up and down. Yes, there are days when you don't want to talk to a soul and other days when you have to be physically prised off the phone. You might think that's just you, but other people call it moodiness. They can also find it hard to keep track of your opinions because you tend to change them quite often. Some people are wedded to their ideas through thick and thin; yours fluctuate according to the circumstances and the time of day. It's all part of what makes you such an interesting person to have around.

Relationships

You belong to the Air element, so you are happiest when dealing with ideas. Emotions make you feel uncomfortable and it can be hard for you to express your feelings. You have just as many feelings as anyone else, but you aren't very happy dealing with them. They can make you embarrassed, tongue-tied and hemmed in. Because you have such a gift for words you can describe your emotions in an intellectual way but it is another story when it comes to experiencing and living them. Anyone who wears their heart on their sleeve makes you wince and want to rush off in the opposite direction.

Even so, your popularity rating is usually sky-high. People adore your sunny nature, your ready laugh and your fascinating conversation. When looking for friends and lovers, you seek out people who are on the same intellectual wavelength as yourself and who make you think. No matter how devastatingly attractive someone is, you won't be with them for long if they're boring, not very bright or don't have a sense of humour. You will soon have other fish to fry.

Money

Money is like a conjuring trick for you. Now you see it, now you don't. You can spend it as soon as you get it! You like to tell yourself that finance doesn't mean much to you and there are more important things in life than having a healthy bank balance or a portfolio of shares, yet you certainly enjoy the things that money can buy. Finance in itself might bore you to tears but if you turn it into an intellectual game you can become absolutely fascinated. For instance, you'll enjoy reading the business pages of newspapers in the same way you read a gossip column – 'Hey, did you see that Knitted Socks Incorporated has just paid $6 billion for Global Mouthwash? I wonder if they'll buy Earplugs United next?' – although the latest movements in your bank account might be a complete mystery to you. Overdrawn? Are you really? How on earth did that happen? It couldn't have anything to do with that pile of clothes you just bought, could it?

Health

You may give the impression of being game for anything and ready to stay up all night, but underneath it all you have a very sensitive nervous system. You are like a clock that looks sturdy and reliable but which goes wrong whenever the mechanism gets out of balance. One of the easiest ways for your system to go wrong is if you are bored. If you go through a period when your life becomes mundane and unexciting, it can make you feel quite ill. When this happens you need to find positive outlets for your nervous energy, such as tennis which is the perfect Gemini sport. You certainly like it when life is busy and lively, although too many late nights will soon catch up with you. So will the typical Gemini diet of too much coffee and cigarettes and not enough solid food.

Most signs fight the battle of the bulge, but many Geminis suffer from the opposite problem and find it difficult to gain weight. It's a problem that makes other signs go green with envy!

Gemini rules the arms, hands and chest, so these are the most vulnerable areas of your body. If you're a typical Gemini you gesticulate all the time while talking – even on the phone – so it's hardly surprising that occasionally these limbs make contact with something hard and the result is a bruise, strain or even a fracture.

Career

Communicating with others is second nature to you, so it's wise to find a career in which this is an essential ingredient. You might find it a struggle to become a Trappist monk or to do anything else that involves long periods of silence. You're simply not cut out for that quiet a life! It's easy for you to get on well with your colleagues and clients – they warm to your breezy personality and you enjoy getting to know them as people in their own right. This natural ability to communicate makes you an ideal candidate for any job in the media, communications industry, advertising or sales. You also need a job that keeps you busy, with plenty of variation in your daily schedule and, ideally, the chance to go travelling. Because you find it easy to do at least two things at once, or to tackle several projects at one time, and to switch between them according to your mood, self-employment may also suit you.

THE MOON AND YOUR RELATIONSHIPS

For centuries the Moon has been worshipped as a goddess, and many myths have tried to explain the Moon's phases, from New to Full and back again. Some of these myths continue today, although you might not realize it. For instance, as children we are taught to look for the Man in the Moon and we recite the nursery rhyme about the cow jumping over the Moon.

Although the Moon is really a satellite of the Earth, astrologers refer to her as a planet. And of all the ten known planets in the solar system, the Moon is the easiest for us to look at. It is dangerous to stare at the Sun and you have to know where to look in the sky to find Venus, Mars, Jupiter and Saturn, all of which are visible to the naked eye when they are above the horizon. But the Moon is our almost constant nightly companion. She vanishes from the sky at the time of a New Moon, only to emerge two days later as a tiny crescent of light – a luminous nail-paring hanging in the sky.

In astrology, the Moon is said to be one of the two lights of the chart – the Sun is the other one. The Moon represents our emotions, instinctive reactions, intuition, habits, what nurtures us, comforts us and feels familiar to us. She also describes our childhood and our relationship with our mother. Therefore, she has a very powerful effect on our relationships, and her position in a birth chart is a very sensitive area. She is a very important planet for everyone but has particular significance for Cancerians because the Moon rules the sign of Cancer.

The Moon is the fastest moving planet in our solar system. She zips through a sign every two-and-a-half days, and takes 29 days to move through her lunation cycle of New to Full to New Moon again. This means it is easy to track her progress through your chart each month, and to see how she affects you emotionally.

If you've always wondered how astrology works, here's a brief explanation. Your horoscope (a map of the planets' positions at the time of your birth) is divided up into twelve sections, known as 'houses'. Each one represents a different area of your life, and together they cover every aspect of our experiences on Earth. As the Moon moves around the heavens each month she progresses through each house in turn, affecting a particular part of your life, such as your health or career. If you plot her progress through your own chart, you'll be able to make the most of the Moon's influence in 2001. That way, you'll know when to concentrate on your relationships with workmates, family, friends and lovers, and also when you may prefer your own company.

To plot the Moon's progress in 2001, fill in the diagram on page 114, writing '1' in the section next to your Sun sign, then numbering consecutively in an anticlockwise direction around the signs until you have completed them all. It will now be easy to chart the Moon's movements. When she is in the same sign as your Sun, the Moon is in your first house. When she moves into the next sign she occupies your second house, and so on, until she reaches your twelfth house, at which point she will move back into your first house again.

Diagram 1

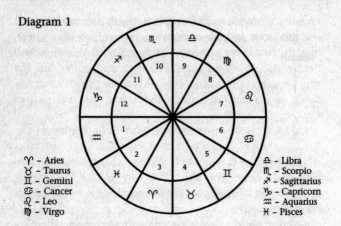

♈ – Aries
♉ – Taurus
♊ – Gemini
♋ – Cancer
♌ – Leo
♍ – Virgo

♎ – Libra
♏ – Scorpio
♐ – Sagittarius
♑ – Capricorn
♒ – Aquarius
♓ – Pisces

Here are the houses of the horoscope, numbered from one to twelve, for someone born with the Sun in Aquarius.

Diagram 2

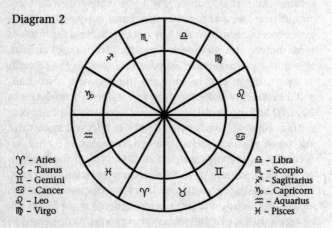

♈ – Aries
♉ – Taurus
♊ – Gemini
♋ – Cancer
♌ – Leo
♍ – Virgo

♎ – Libra
♏ – Scorpio
♐ – Sagittarius
♑ – Capricorn
♒ – Aquarius
♓ – Pisces

Fill in the blank diagram, writing '1' in the section next to your Sun sign. Working in an anticlockwise direction, write '2' in the next section and so on, until you have filled in all twelve sections.

THE MOON'S ENTRY INTO THE SIGNS IN 2001
(All times are given in GMT, using the 24-hour clock)

January

1	Pisces	00:00
1	Aries	22:15
4	Taurus	06:58
6	Gemini	11:45
8	Cancer	13:10
10	Leo	12:45
12	Virgo	12:27
14	Libra	14:06
16	Scorpio	19:03
19	Sagittarius	03:37
21	Capricorn	14:58
24	Aquarius	03:44
26	Pisces	16:40
29	Aries	04:36
31	Taurus	14:22

February

1	Taurus	00:00
2	Gemini	20:57
5	Cancer	00:01
7	Leo	00:22
8	Virgo	23:36
10	Libra	23:47
13	Scorpio	02:52
15	Sagittarius	10:03
17	Capricorn	21:00
20	Aquarius	09:55
22	Pisces	22:46
25	Aries	10:21
27	Taurus	20:07

March

1	Taurus	00:00
2	Gemini	03:37
4	Cancer	08:25
6	Leo	10:31
8	Virgo	10:45
10	Libra	10:48
12	Scorpio	12:44
14	Sagittarius	18:18
17	Capricorn	04:03
19	Aquarius	16:37
22	Pisces	05:29
24	Aries	16:45
27	Taurus	01:52
29	Gemini	09:02
31	Cancer	14:24

April

1	Cancer	00:00
2	Leo	17:55
4	Virgo	19:48
6	Libra	20:58
8	Scorpio	23:02
11	Sagittarius	03:48
13	Capricorn	12:22
16	Aquarius	00:12
18	Pisces	13:01
21	Aries	00:19
23	Taurus	08:57
25	Gemini	15:12
27	Cancer	19:50
29	Leo	23:26

May		
1	Leo	00:00
2	Virgo	02:17
4	Libra	04:51
6	Scorpio	08:02
8	Sagittarius	13:06
10	Capricorn	21:11
13	Aquarius	08:21
15	Pisces	21:02
18	Aries	08:42
20	Taurus	17:30
22	Gemini	23:13
25	Cancer	02:43
27	Leo	05:13
29	Virgo	07:39
31	Libra	10:42

June		
1	Libra	00:00
2	Scorpio	14:57
4	Sagittarius	20:59
7	Capricorn	05:24
9	Aquarius	16:21
12	Pisces	04:54
14	Aries	17:04
17	Taurus	02:40
19	Gemini	08:43
21	Cancer	11:42
23	Leo	12:56
25	Virgo	13:59
27	Libra	16:12
29	Scorpio	20:30

July		
1	Scorpio	00:00
2	Sagittarius	03:14
4	Capricorn	12:23
6	Aquarius	23:34
9	Pisces	12:06
12	Aries	00:37
14	Taurus	11:14
16	Gemini	18:27
18	Cancer	21:57
20	Leo	22:44
22	Virgo	22:30
24	Libra	23:09
27	Scorpio	02:18
29	Sagittarius	08:45
31	Capricorn	18:17

August		
1	Capricorn	00:00
3	Aquarius	05:54
5	Pisces	18:31
8	Aries	07:06
10	Taurus	18:24
13	Gemini	03:00
15	Cancer	07:56
17	Leo	09:26
19	Virgo	08:54
21	Libra	08:20
23	Scorpio	09:51
25	Sagittarius	15:00
28	Capricorn	00:03
30	Aquarius	11:49

September

1	Aquarius	00:00
2	Pisces	00:33
4	Aries	12:59
7	Taurus	00:19
9	Gemini	09:42
11	Cancer	16:10
13	Leo	19:17
15	Virgo	19:40
17	Libra	19:01
19	Scorpio	19:28
21	Sagittarius	23:03
24	Capricorn	06:49
26	Aquarius	18:06
29	Pisces	06:51

October

1	Pisces	00:00
1	Aries	19:09
4	Taurus	06:02
6	Gemini	15:13
8	Cancer	22:20
11	Leo	02:55
13	Virgo	04:59
15	Libra	05:27
17	Scorpio	06:04
19	Sagittarius	08:48
21	Capricorn	15:12
24	Aquarius	01:27
26	Pisces	13:57
29	Aries	02:16
31	Taurus	12:49

November

1	Taurus	00:00
2	Gemini	21:14
5	Cancer	03:45
7	Leo	08:35
9	Virgo	11:50
11	Libra	13:54
13	Scorpio	15:46
15	Sagittarius	18:52
18	Capricorn	00:41
20	Aquarius	09:56
22	Pisces	21:53
25	Aries	10:22
27	Taurus	21:07
30	Gemini	05:05

December

1	Gemini	00:00
2	Cancer	10:31
4	Leo	14:17
6	Virgo	17:12
8	Libra	19:58
10	Scorpio	23:10
13	Sagittarius	03:31
15	Capricorn	09:49
17	Aquarius	18:44
20	Pisces	06:10
22	Aries	18:46
25	Taurus	06:13
27	Gemini	14:40
29	Cancer	19:41
31	Leo	22:10

The Moon in the First House

You are very wrapped up in yourself at the moment because your own emotional needs take precedence over everyone else's. It is a good opportunity to think about what and who makes you happy, and also to focus on whatever you need right now. However, this can cause problems because other people may regard you as being self-centred. They might even accuse you of being selfish. What do you do about this? If you live alone you might choose to spend most of this lunar phase by yourself, perhaps writing your diary. If you live with someone, you may have to compromise and make yourself pay attention to the other person, giving them the chance to talk about what is important rather than hogging all the limelight yourself.

The Moon in the Second House

When the Moon is in this part of your chart you are happiest if you can concentrate on whatever and whoever means the most to you in life. In an ideal world, you would screen out other distractions and only concentrate on your priorities in life when the Moon was in your second house. Even if that isn't possible, it is certainly a good excuse to get together with some of the people you care about most because you will really appreciate their company. All the same, watch out for a possible tendency to become rather possessive, making you behave as though loved ones are your personal property or you can't bear to let them do anything without you. This is a good time to talk to people who can give you financial advice.

The Moon in the Third House

This is one of the liveliest times of the entire month for you. You are in the mood to communicate with whoever happens to be around, so it's a wonderful chance to make the most of your social life. You may be particularly drawn to close relatives such as brothers and sisters, neighbours and other people that you see on a regular basis. You will enjoy discussing ideas but you will also be keen to hear the latest gossip. Even so, make sure that everyone gets a chance to have their say, because you may get carried away and want to chat nineteen to the dozen. If there has been a problem recently with someone that you know well, this is the perfect opportunity to patch up your differences.

The Moon in the Fourth House

Family matters are dear to your heart at this point in the lunar calendar. You may feel rather nostalgic for times gone past and you might even enjoy looking through keepsakes or old photos. It's the perfect chance to get together with relatives and also with very close friends who feel like family. You will enjoy being with people who know you inside out. In fact, you may feel uncomfortable if you have to meet anyone for the first time because you are much more relaxed when surrounded by familiar faces at the moment. You are feeling very protective of your loved ones and will want to take care of them. You might decide to cook someone a delicious meal or do something that makes you feel cosy, such as baking a cake.

The Moon in the Fifth House

This is one of the times of the month when you really want to enjoy yourself. It's ideal for getting together with some of your favourite people because you will appreciate having them around. You are in the mood for love, laughter and a lot of fun, so try to surround yourself with people who feel the same way. Remind them of how much you appreciate them. It's a lovely time to be with babies and children, and you will enjoy playing with them. Romance is also in the air now so it's a super time for being with your one true love, or perhaps you will meet someone new. Even if you don't have anyone special in your life, this is a wonderful opportunity to be demonstrative, affectionate and caring to the people you know.

The Moon in the Sixth House

Look after yourself while the Moon is moving through this part of your chart. You may be feeling slightly under par physically. You may also be rather vulnerable when dealing with people who are bossy or who behave as though you are only there to look after their every need. It's a very good time to concentrate on your relationships with colleagues and customers. You have a strong need to be of service to them and also to do your best in your job. You might find yourself listening to someone with a tale of woe or they could ask your advice about something. If you need to visit your doctor or dentist, try to make an appointment for when the Moon is in this part of your chart because you will be very receptive to what they have to say.

The Moon in the Seventh House

Concentrate on your one-to-one relationships while the Moon moves through this part of your chart. That might mean spending time with your other half, your business partner, a friend or a member of the family. You are sympathetic to the feelings of others and you want to foster a sense of harmony between you. It's a marvellous chance to sort out a problem with someone because you will strive to keep the conversation as easy-going and fair as possible. You will ensure that both of you have the chance to air your views. Teamwork is far more successful than going it alone at the moment, so try to work in tandem with other people whenever possible. If you have to spend too long by yourself you may start to feel lonely or neglected.

The Moon in the Eighth House

Prepare yourself for a short bout of intense emotions. Even if you usually pride yourself on keeping your feelings under control, it could be a different story at the moment. You may feel churned up about situations or problems that you realize you have been stewing over for a long time. On rare occasions there could also be flashes of jealousy or suspicion, in which you suspect that a close partner is not being honest with you. However, it is far more likely that you will enjoy a strong rapport with loved ones during this time. It is your chance to become closer to them, to strengthen your understanding of one another and to talk about any problems that exist between you. There may also be some passionate encounters with a certain person!

The Moon in the Ninth House

You long to broaden your horizons while the Moon moves through this part of your chart. You aren't content with ideas and people that are familiar to you – you want to branch out in new directions. Make the most of your current open-minded attitude by talking to people who come from different countries and cultures. You might get involved in a discussion about someone's religious or spiritual beliefs, and you will want to give them a fair hearing even if you don't agree with what they are saying. This is a super time of the month for getting in touch with friends and family who live a long way away, especially if they happen to be overseas. You might also enjoy visiting Internet chat rooms and discussing subjects that fascinate you.

The Moon in the Tenth House

This is a good time to get in touch with older relatives and friends. You will value their wisdom and experience. It's a great opportunity to ask their advice, although you should be prepared for what might be some rather conventional answers. But this isn't only a time to pick people's brains. It's lovely for simply enjoying the company of older people, especially grandparents, and perhaps allowing them to make a fuss of you. You will also find it easy to establish an enjoyable rapport with superiors and anyone else who is in authority over you. So it might be a good move to get chatting to your boss or supervisor at the moment.

The Moon in the Eleventh House

Friends are extra important to you when the Moon moves through this part of your chart. Ideally, you should concentrate on your friendships as much as possible now because they will bring you lots of emotional satisfaction. You might want to get together with your best friend, perhaps having a meal together. You will enjoy being with them because it's comforting that you know one another so well. It also means you don't have to be on your best behaviour with them! However, this is also a very good time to make some new friends. You might decide to join a club or organization that caters for one of your interests, especially if you are hoping to meet some kindred spirits as a result.

The Moon in the Twelfth House

This is the point in the Moon's monthly cycle when you want to wrap yourself in cotton wool and stay away from anyone who can be unpleasant, harsh or critical. That is because you are feeling very sensitive at the moment and it won't take much to hurt you and make you want to retreat into your shell. Try to postpone seeing anyone difficult until a couple of days' time when you are feeling more confident. In the meantime, you will be happiest if you can alternate some much-needed privacy with seeing people that you love and trust. Romance might be in the air, so it's a super opportunity to hide away from the rest of the world with that special person in your life.

LOVE AND THE STARS

All the world loves a lover. And life can seem pretty good when you are in love yourself. You are more tolerant of others and you want everyone else to be as happy as you are. However, as we all know to our cost, love can also cause lots of problems. It can be miserable if you are with the wrong person or you are stuck in a dead-end relationship because it seems a better bet than being left on your own. As with every other area of life, astrology can help you to sort out your love life. If you always end up with a broken heart or you have given up on romance because it seems like such a hassle, maybe this guide could help. And if you are blissfully happy with that special person in your life, this chapter will reveal what your secret is and could also give you some ideas about how to make things even better.

At the end of my astrological guide to love, there are two compatibility charts on pages 144 and 145, so you can see at a glance how you get on with all the Sun signs, as lovers and also as friends. Each combination has been marked out of ten, so you can see whether it's a heaven-sent pairing or more likely to be a disaster from the word go. Ten means it has the potential to be the best thing that ever happened to you, and one means that it's best forgotten about as quickly as possible! Having said that, don't despair if your current relationship gets a low score. Every Sun sign combination stands a chance of success, but some are easier to deal with than others.

All you need to do is look for the woman's Sun sign along the top of the chart and then find the man's sign down the side. The box where the two meet will show how well they get on together.

🚶🚶 Gemini

One of the Air signs, Geminis get on very well with their fellow members of this element – Librans and Aquarians. Two Geminis are the astrological equivalent of double trouble – they chat nineteen to the dozen and revel in the company of someone who understands them so well. A Gemini delights in being with a Libran, because they enjoy the intellectual company and will benefit from the Libran's (usually) relaxed approach to life. They'll also learn to deal with their emotions more if a sympathetic Libran can guide them. Gemini and Aquarius is a very exciting pairing – the Gemini is encouraged to think deeply and knows that the Aquarian won't put up with any woolly ideas or fudged arguments.

Geminis also get on well with the three Fire signs – Aries, Leo and Sagittarius. A Gemini loves being with a racy, adventurous Arien, and together they enjoy keeping abreast of all the latest gossip and cultural developments. However, after the first flush of enthusiasm has worn off, the Gemini may find the Arien's strong need for sex rather hard to take. The Gemini gets on very well with a Leo. They delight in the Leo's affectionate nature and are amused by their need to have the best that money can buy – and they'll gladly share in the spoils. Gemini and Sagittarius are an excellent combination, because they sit opposite each other in the zodiac and so complement one another's character. The Gemini will be fascinated by the erudite and knowledgeable Sagittarian.

Gemini doesn't do so well with the Earth signs of Taurus and Capricorn, although they get on better with Virgo. The Gemini finds it difficult to understand a Taurean, because they see the world from such different viewpoints. The Gemini takes a more light-hearted approach and lives life at such a speed that they find it difficult to slow down to the more measured pace of a Taurean. The wonderfully dry Capricorn sense of humour is a source of constant delight to a Gemini. However, they're less taken with the Capricorn's streak of pessimism and their love of tradition. Of the three Earth signs, Gemini and Virgo are the most compatible. The Gemini shares the Virgo's brainpower and they have long, fascinating conversations.

When a Gemini gets together with the Water signs, the result can be enjoyable or puzzling. Gemini and Cancer have little in common, because the Gemini wants to spread their emotional and intellectual wings, whereas a Cancerian likes to stay close to home and has little interest in abstract ideas. Gemini finds Scorpio perplexing because they operate on such different levels. A Gemini tends to skim along the surface of things, so often deals with life on a superficial level, whereas a Scorpio likes to dig deep and has to have an emotional investment in everything they do. A Gemini appreciates the subtlety and sensitivity of a Piscean, but they're likely to make off-the-cuff comments that unwittingly hurt the Piscean.

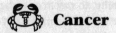 **Cancer**

Cancerians revel in the company of their fellow Water signs of Scorpio and Pisces. When two Cancerians get together they could spend most of their time at home or eating – preferably both. They feel safe in the knowledge that they both have a strong need for love, but their innate Cancerian tenacity may mean they cling on to the relationship even if it's long past its best. A Cancerian is enchanted with a Scorpio, because at last they feel free to really let rip emotionally. However, the intuitive Cancerian should beware of soaking up the Scorpio's darker moods like a psychic sponge. A Cancerian will take one look at a delicate Piscean and want to invite them home for a good hot meal. All the Cancerian's protective instincts are aroused by a gentle Piscean, but their anger will also be aroused if it turns out the Piscean has been leading a double life behind their back.

Cancerians also find a great deal of comfort in the company of the Earth signs – Taurus, Virgo and Capricorn. Cancer and Taurus were made for each other – they both adore home comforts and they trust one another implicitly. The Cancerian loves making a cosy nest for their hard-working Taurean. A Cancerian finds a Virgo a more difficult proposition, especially emotionally. Whereas Cancer is all warm hugs and holding hands by the fire, Virgo prefers to read a book and reserve any displays of affection for the bedroom. Cancer and Capricorn are opposite numbers in the zodiac, so share a tremendous rapport. They also share the same values of home, tradition and family, and if anyone can help a Capricorn to relax and take life easy, it's a Cancerian.

Life becomes more difficult when it comes to a Cancerian's relationship with any of the Air signs. They simply don't understand one another. A Cancerian can't make a Gemini out. They feel confused by what they think of as the Gemini's flightiness and inability to stay in one place for long. They can also be easily hurt by the Gemini's difficulty in expressing their emotions. A Cancerian gets on much better with a Libran. They're both ambitious in their own ways and so have a great deal in common. The Cancerian enjoys the Libran's romantic nature, but the Cancerian tendency to cling doesn't go down well. A Cancerian regards a typical Aquarian as a being from another planet. They're hurt by the Aquarian's strong need for independence and dislike of having to account for their every action, and are dismayed and confused by the Aquarian's hot-and-cold attitude to sex.

The Fire signs of Aries, Leo and Sagittarius are also a potential source of bewilderment to the gentle Cancerian. They understand the drive and ambition of an Arien, but will be stung by their blunt speech and worried about their daredevil tendencies. What if they hurt themselves? A Cancerian gets on well with a Leo because they share a strong love of family and are both openly affectionate and loving. The Cancerian enjoys creating a home that the Leo can feel proud of. So far, so good, but the story isn't so simple when a Cancerian pairs up with a Sagittarian. They're too different to understand one another – the Cancerian wants to stay at home with the family while the Sagittarian has an instinctive need to roam the world. As a result, the Cancerian will be disappointed, and then hurt, when the Sagittarian's busy schedule takes them away from home too often.

 Leo

Leos adore the company of their fellow Fire signs, Ariens and Sagittarius. They understand one another and enjoy each other's spontaneous warmth and affection. A Leo is amused by the exuberance and impulsiveness of an Arien, and they enjoy being persuaded to let their hair down a bit and not worry too much about appearances. A Leo enjoys the dash and vitality of a Sagittarian, although they may feel irritated if they can never get hold of them on the phone or the Sagittarian is always off doing other things. Two Leos together either love or loathe one another. One of them should be prepared to take a back seat, otherwise they'll both be vying for the limelight all the time.

The three Air signs of Gemini, Libra and Aquarius all get on well with Leos. When a Leo pairs up with a Gemini, you can expect lots of laughter and plenty of fascinating conversations. The demonstrative Leo is able to help the Gemini be more openly affectionate and loving. Leo and Libra is a great combination, and the Leo is enchanted by the Libran's fair-minded attitude. Both signs love luxury and all the good things in life but their bank managers may not be so pleased by the amount of the money they manage to spend. Leo and Aquarius sit opposite one another across the horoscope, so they already have a great deal in common. They're fascinated by one another but they're both very stubborn, so any disputes between them usually end in stalemate because neither is prepared to concede any ground.

Leos don't really understand the Earth signs. Although Leos admire their practical approach to life, they find it rather restricting. A Leo enjoys the sensuous and hedonistic side of a Taurean's character but may become frustrated by their fear of change. Leo and Virgo have very little in common, especially when it comes to food – the Leo wants to tuck in at all the best restaurants while the Virgo is worried about the state of the kitchens, the number of calories and the size of the bill. A Leo respects the Capricorn's desire to support their family and approves of their need to be seen in the best possible light, but they feel hurt by the Capricorn's difficulty in showing their feelings.

When a Leo gets together with one of the Water signs – Cancer, Scorpio or Pisces – they'll enjoy the sexual side of the relationship but could eventually feel stifled by all that Watery emotion. A Leo and a Cancerian adore making a home together and both dote on their children. The Leo also likes comforting their vulnerable Cancerian – provided this doesn't happen too often. A Leo and a Scorpio will be powerfully attracted to one another, but power could also pull them apart – who's going to wear the trousers? They'll also lock horns during rows and both of them will refuse to back down. A Leo delights in a sophisticated Piscean, but may become irritated by their indecision and jangly nerves.

Virgo

As you might imagine, Virgos are happy with their fellow Earth signs of Taurus and Capricorn because they share the same practical attitude. A Virgo enjoys the steady, reassuring company of a Taurean, and they might even learn to relax a little instead of worrying themselves into the ground over the slightest problem. When two Virgos get together it can be too much of a good thing. Although at first they'll love talking to someone who shares so many of their preoccupations and ideas, they can soon drive one another round the bend. When a Virgo first meets a Capricorn they're delighted to know someone who's obviously got their head screwed on. It's only later on that they wish the Capricorn could lighten up every now and then.

Virgos get on well with Cancerians, Scorpios and Pisceans, the three Water signs. A Virgo enjoys being looked after by a considerate Cancerian, although they'll worry about their waistline and may get irritated by the Cancerian's super-sensitive feelings. You can expect plenty of long, analytical conversations when a Virgo gets together with a Scorpio. They both love getting to the bottom of subjects and will endlessly talk things through. They'll also get on extremely well in the bedroom. Pisces is Virgo's opposite sign, but although some opposites thrive in each other's company, that isn't always the case with this combination. The Virgo could soon grow impatient with the dreamy Piscean and will long to tell them a few home truths.

Although the other Earth signs don't usually get on well with Air signs, it's different for Virgos. They understand the intellectual energies of Geminis, Librans and Aquarians. A Virgo thrives in a Gemini's company, and they spend hours chatting over the phone if they can't get together in person. It's difficult for them to discuss their emotions, however, and they may never tell each other how they really feel. A Virgo admires a sophisticated, charming Libran, and marvels at their diplomacy. How do they do it? Expect a few sparks to fly when a Virgo pairs up with an Aquarian, because both of them have very strong opinions and aren't afraid to air them. The result is a lot of hot air and some vigorous arguments.

The three Fire signs – Aries, Leo and Sagittarius – are a source of endless fascination to a Virgo. They've got so much energy! A Virgo finds an Arien exciting but their relationship could be short-lived because the Virgo will be so irritated by the Arien's devil-may-care attitude to life. When a Virgo pairs up with a Leo, they'll be intrigued by this person's comparatively lavish lifestyle but their own modest temperament will be shocked if the Leo enjoys showing off. A Virgo is able to talk to a Sagittarius until the cows come home – they're both fascinated by ideas, although the precise Virgo will first be amused, and then irritated, by the Sagittarian's rather relaxed attitude to hard facts.

Libra

Of all the members of the zodiac, this is the one that finds it easiest to get on with the other signs. Librans get on particularly well with Geminis and Aquarians, their fellow Air signs. A Libran is enchanted by a Gemini's quick brain and ready wit, and they enjoy endless discussions on all sorts of subjects. When two Librans get together, they revel in the resulting harmonious atmosphere but it's almost impossible for them to reach any decisions – each one defers to the other while being unable to say what they really want. A Libran is intrigued by the independence and sharp mind of an Aquarian, but their feelings could be hurt by the Aquarian's emotional coolness.

Libra enjoys being with the three Fire signs – Aries, Leo and Sagittarius. Libra, who often takes life at rather a slow pace, is energized by a lively Arien, and they complement one another's personalities well. However, the Libran may occasionally feel hurt by the Arien's single-mindedness and blunt speech. A Libran adores the luxury-loving ways of a Leo, and they'll both spend a fortune in the pursuit of happiness. They also get on well in the bedroom. When a Libran gets together with an exuberant Sagittarian, they'll have great fun. All the same, the Sagittarian need for honesty could fluster the Libran, who adopts a much more diplomatic approach to life.

Although the other two Air signs can find it hard to understand members of the Water element, it's different for Librans. They're more sympathetic to the emotional energies of Cancerians, Scorpios and Pisceans. A Libran delights in the protective care of a Cancerian, but those ever-changing Cancerian moods may be hard for a balanced Libran to take. Those deep Scorpio emotions will intrigue the Libran but they may quickly become bogged down by such an intense outlook on life and will be desperate for some light relief. As for Pisces, the Libran is charmed by the Piscean's delicate nature and creative gifts, but both signs hate facing up to unpleasant facts so this couple may never deal with any problems that lie between them.

Libra enjoys the reliable natures of Taurus, Virgo and Capricorn, the Earth signs. A Libran appreciates the company of a relaxed and easy-going Taurean, although they may sometimes regret the Taurean's lack of imagination. When a Libran and a Virgo get together, the Libran enjoys the Virgo's mental abilities but their critical comments will soon cut the Libran to the quick. The Libran may not come back for a second tongue-lashing. A Libran understands the ambitions of a Capricorn, and likes their steady nature and the way they support their family. However, there could soon be rows about money, with the Libran spending a lot more than the Capricorn thinks is necessary.

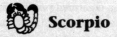 **Scorpio**

Not every sign gets on well with its fellow members, yet an astonishing number of Scorpios pair up. They feel safe together because they know the worst and best about each other. When things are good, they're brilliant but these two can also bring out the worst in each other, with intense silences and brooding sulks. A Scorpio enjoys the tender ministrations of a loving Cancerian, and adores being with someone who's so obviously concerned about their welfare. Feelings run deep when a Scorpio pairs up with a Piscean, although the Scorpio may become impatient with the Piscean's reluctance to face up to unpalatable truths.

The three Earth signs – Taurus, Virgo and Capricorn – are well-suited to the Scorpio temperament. Those astrological opposites, Scorpio and Taurus, enjoy a powerful relationship, much of which probably takes place in the bedroom, but whenever they have a disagreement there's an atmosphere you could cut with a knife, and neither of them will be prepared to admit they were in the wrong. A Scorpio is attracted to a neat, analytical Virgo but their feelings will be hurt by this sign's tendency to criticize. What's more, their pride stops them telling the Virgo how they feel. The Scorpio admires a practical Capricorn, especially if they've earned a lot of respect through their work, but this could be a rather chilly pairing because both signs find it difficult to show their feelings.

When you put a Scorpio together with one of the three Fire

signs, they'll either get on famously or won't understand one another at all. A Scorpio revels in the lusty Arien's sex drive, although they'll soon feel tired if they try to keep up with the Arien's busy schedule. The combination of Scorpio and Leo packs quite a punch. They're both very strong personalities, but they boss one another around like mad and find it almost impossible to achieve a compromise if they fall out. A Scorpio likes to take life at a measured pace, so they're bemused by a Sagittarian's need to keep busy all the time. In the end, they'll become fed up with never seeing the Sagittarian, or playing second fiddle to all their other interests.

Scorpio is bemused by the three Air signs – Gemini, Libra and Aquarius – because they operate on such completely different wavelengths. A Scorpio can be good friends with a Gemini but they're at emotional cross-purposes, with the Scorpio's intense approach to life too much for a light-hearted Gemini to cope with. Emotions are also the bugbear between a Scorpio and a Libran. Everything is great at first, but the Scorpio's powerful feelings and dark moods will eventually send the Libran running in the opposite direction. You can expect some tense arguments when a Scorpio pairs up with an Aquarian – they're both convinced that they're right and the other one is wrong.

♐ Sagittarius

When a Sagittarian pairs up with a fellow Fire sign, there's plenty of warmth and the odd firework. A Sagittarian is thrilled by the adventurous spirit of an Arien, and they love exploring the world together. There are plenty of tall tales when a Sagittarian gets together with a Leo – they'll try to outdo each other, dropping names and recounting their greatest triumphs. If the Leo is slightly pompous, the Sagittarian is able to take them down a peg or two, but they must beware of hurting the Leo's feelings. As for two Sagittarians, they'll spur each other on and encourage one another to gain as much experience of life as possible. You probably won't be able to move in their house for books.

With their endless curiosity about the world, Sagittarians understand the intellectual Air signs very well. A Sagittarian enjoys the chatty company of a Gemini and, because they're opposite numbers in the zodiac, the Sagittarian is able to encourage the Gemini to see things through and explore them in more detail than usual. A refined and diplomatic Libran will try to teach the blunt Sagittarian not to say the first thing that pops into their head. However, the Sagittarian may eventually find the Libran's sense of balance rather trying – why can't they get more worked up about things? There's plenty of straight talking when a Sagittarian teams up with an Aquarian – they both have a high regard for honesty. The independent Sagittarian respects the Aquarian's need for freedom, but may feel rather stung by their periods of emotional coolness.

A Sagittarian will struggle to understand the Earth signs. They respect the Taurean's ability to work hard but they're driven to distraction by their reluctance to make changes and break out of any ruts they've fallen into. A Sagittarian enjoys talking to a brainy Virgo, but their expansive and spontaneous nature could eventually be restricted by the Virgo's need to think things through before taking action. When a Sagittarian gets together with a Capricorn, it's a case of optimism versus pessimism. While the Sagittarian's glass is half-full, the Capricorn's is always half-empty, and this causes many rows and possibly some ill feeling.

There could be lots of misunderstandings when a Sagittarian gets involved with one of the Water signs. A Sagittarian needs a bigger social circle than their family, whereas a Cancerian is quite happy surrounded by kith and kin. The Sagittarian need for independence won't go down well, either. It's like oil and water when a Sagittarian pairs up with a Scorpio. The Sagittarian is the roamer of the zodiac, whereas the Scorpio wants them where they can see them, in case they're up to no good. All will be well if the Sagittarian gets together with a strong-minded Piscean. In fact, they'll really enjoy one another's company. A Piscean who's lost in a world of their own, however, will soon leave them cold.

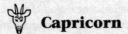

Capricorn

Despite their outward poise, a Capricorn is very easily hurt so they need to know their feelings won't be trampled on. There's least danger of that when they get together with a fellow Earth sign. A Capricorn adores a Taurean's deep sense of responsibility and they'll both work hard to create their ideal home. A Capricorn appreciates the methodical approach of a Virgo, but could feel deeply hurt by the Virgo's sharp tongue and caustic remarks. If two Capricorns team up, one of them must be demonstrative and openly affectionate, otherwise the relationship could be rather sterile and serious.

Capricorns also feel safe with members of the Water signs. When a Capricorn gets together with a Cancerian, they do their utmost to make their home a haven. They'll get great satisfaction from channelling their energies into bringing up a family. A Capricorn may be rather bemused by the depth and intensity of a Scorpio's emotions – Capricorns are too reserved to indulge in such drama themselves and it can make them feel uncomfortable. A no-nonsense Capricorn could be per-plexed by an extremely vulnerable Piscean and won't know how to handle them. Should they give them a hanky or tell them to pull themselves together?

The Air signs can also make a Capricorn feel somewhat unsettled. They're fascinated by a Gemini's breadth of knowl-edge and endless chat, but they also find them superficial and rather flighty. In fact, the Capricorn probably doesn't trust the Gemini. A Capricorn feels far. happier in the company of a Libran. Here's someone who seems much steadier emotionally and who can help the Capricorn to unwind after a hard day's work. It can be great or ghastly when a Capricorn sets their sights on an Aquarian. They understand each other provided the Aquarian isn't too unconventional, but the Capricorn feels uncomfortable and embarrassed by any displays of eccentricity, deliberate or not.

The Fire signs help to warm up the Capricorn, who can be rather remote and distant at times. A Capricorn admires the Arien's drive and initiative, but endlessly tells them to look before they leap and could become irritated when they don't take this sage advice. When a Capricorn gets together with a Leo, they won't need to worry about appearances – the Capricorn will feel justly proud of the smart Leo. However, they could wince when the bills come in and they discover how much those clothes cost. A Capricorn thinks a Sagittarian must have come from another planet – how can they be so relaxed and laid-back all the time? They have great respect for the Sagittarian's wisdom and philosophy, but they quickly become fed up with having to fit in around the Sagittarian's hectic social life.

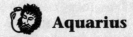 **Aquarius**

Put an Aquarian with a fellow Air sign and they're happy. They thoroughly enjoy being with a lively Gemini and love discussing everything under the sun with them. They may not have a very exciting sex life, but their mental closeness will more than make up for it. The gentle charm of a Libran calms down an Aquarian when their nerves become frayed, although they disapprove of the Libran's innate tact and diplomacy – why can't they just say what they think, instead of sitting on the fence? With two Aquarians you never know what to expect, other than that they'll be great friends. They'll certainly do a lot of talking, but could spend more time debating esoteric ideas and abstract concepts.

An Aquarian likes all the Fire signs, although they find Ariens hard to fathom and can become exhausted by an Arien's endless supply of energy and enthusiasm. There are no such problems when an Aquarian pairs up with a Leo because they complement each other in many ways. The Aquarian teaches objectivity to the Leo, who in return encourages the Aquarian to express their emotions more. An Aquarian thoroughly enjoys being with a Sagittarian because both of them hate being tied down. As a result, they respect one another's independence and will probably rarely see each other because of all their spare-time activities.

It's not quite so simple when an Aquarian joins forces with one of the Earth signs. An Aquarian will lock horns with a Taurean sooner or later, because neither of them is able to back down once a disagreement has started. The Aquarian will also feel very restricted by the Taurean's possessiveness. The Virgo's analytical approach to life intrigues the Aquarian but they'll sit up all night arguing the toss over everything, with each one convinced that they've got all the answers. When an Aquarian meets a Capricorn, they've got their work cut out for them if they're to find a happy medium between the erratic Aquarian and the conventional Capricorn.

An Aquarian feels out of their depth when they're with one of the Water signs. They simply don't understand what makes a Cancerian tick – why do they worry themselves sick over things that they can't change? The Aquarian finds it all most peculiar. They also find it difficult to understand a Scorpio who takes so many things so seriously. Although the Aquarian also has a list of topics that mean a lot to them, they're not the sort of things that hold the slightest interest for a Scorpio. It's more or less the same story with a Pisces, because their huge resources of emotion make the Aquarian feel uncomfortable and fill them with a strong desire to escape as fast as possible.

 **Pisces**

Relationships mean a lot to a sensitive Piscean, but they're easily misunderstood by many of the more robust signs. There are no such worries with the other Water signs, however. A Piscean loves being with a tender Cancerian who knows how to help them relax and feel safe. They really enjoy playing house together but the emotional scenes will blow the roof off. The relationship between a Piscean and a Scorpio can be quite spicy and sexy, but the Piscean is turned off if the Scorpio becomes too intense and dramatic. Two Pisceans feel safe with one another, but they'll push all their problems under the carpet unless one of them is more objective.

A Piscean also gets on well with the Earth signs, although with a few reservations. A Piscean takes comfort from being looked after by a protective Taurean, but after a while they could feel stifled by the Taurean's possessive and matter-of-fact attitude. The relationship between a Piscean and a Virgo starts off well but the Piscean could soon feel crushed by the Virgo's criticism and will need more emotional reassurance than the Virgo is able to give. A Piscean feels safe with a Capricorn because they're so dependable but in the end this may begin to bug them. It's not that they want the Capricorn to two-time them, more that they'd like a little unpredictability every now and then.

A Piscean is fascinated by the Air signs but their apparent lack of emotion could cause problems. A Piscean and a Gemini are terrific friends but could encounter difficulties as lovers. The Piscean's strong emotional needs are too much for the Gemini to handle – they'll feel as if they're drowning. The

Piscean is on much firmer ground with a Libran, who'll go out of their way to keep the Piscean happy. Neither sign is good at facing up to any nasty truths, however. An Aquarian is too much for a sensitive Piscean, who views the world through rose-coloured specs. An Aquarian, on the other hand, has uncomfortably clear vision.

The Fire signs can cheer up a Piscean enormously, but any prolonged displays of emotion will make the Fire signs feel weighed down. The Piscean is fascinated by an Arien's exploits but could feel reluctant to join in. They'll also be easily hurt by some of the Arien's off-the-cuff remarks. When a Piscean pairs up with a Leo they appreciate the way the Leo wants to take charge and look after them. After a while, however, this could grate on them and they'll want to be more independent. A Piscean enjoys discussing philosophy and spiritual ideas with a Sagittarian – they can sit up half the night talking things through. The Sagittarian brand of honesty could hurt the Piscean at times, but they know this isn't malicious and will quickly forgive such outbursts.

 Aries

Because Ariens belong to the Fire element, they get on very well with their fellow Fire signs Leo and Sagittarius. All the same, an Arien getting together with a Leo will soon notice a distinct drop in their bank balance, because they'll enjoy going to all the swankiest restaurants and sitting in the best seats at the theatre. When an Arien pairs up with a Sagittarian, they'll compete over who drives the fastest car and has the most exciting holidays. When two Ariens get together the results can be combustible. Ideally, one Arien should be a lot quieter, otherwise they'll spend most of their time jostling for power. All these combinations are very sexy and physical.

Ariens also thrive in the company of the three Air signs – Gemini, Libra and Aquarius. Of the three, they get on best with Geminis, who share their rather childlike view of the world and also their sense of fun. An Arien and a Gemini enjoy hatching all sorts of ideas and schemes, even if they never get round to putting them into action. There's an exciting sense of friction between Aries and Libra, their opposite number in the zodiac. An Arien will be enchanted by the way their Libran caters to their every need, but may become impatient when the Libran also wants to look after other people. An Arien will be captivated by the originality of an Aquarian, although at times they'll be driven mad by the Aquarian's eccentric approach to life and the way they blow hot and cold in the bedroom.

Ariens don't do so well with the Earth signs – Taurus, Virgo and Capricorn. The very careful, slightly plodding nature of a typical Taurean can drive an Arien barmy at times, and although they'll respect – and benefit from – the Taurean's practical approach to life, it can still fill them with irritation. An Arien finds it difficult to fathom a Virgo, because their attitudes to life are diametrically opposed. An Arien likes to jump in with both feet, while a Virgo prefers to take things slowly and analyze every possibility before committing themselves. An Arien can get on quite well with a Capricorn, because they're linked by their sense of ambition and their earthy sexual needs.

An Arien is out of their depth with any of the Water signs – Cancer, Scorpio and Pisces. They quickly become irritated by the defensive Cancerian, although they'll love their cooking. An Arien will enjoy a very passionate affair with a Scorpio, but the Scorpio's need to know exactly what the Arien is up to when their back is turned will soon cause problems and rifts. Although an Arien may begin a relationship with a Pisces by wanting to look after them and protect them from the harsh realities of life, eventually the Piscean's extremely sensitive nature may bring out the Arien's bullying streak.

🐂 Taurus

Taureans are literally in their element when they're with Virgos or Capricorns who, like themselves, are Earth signs. Two Taureans will get along very happily together, although they could become so wedded to routine that they get stuck in a rut. They may also encourage one another to eat too much. A Taurean will enjoy being with a Virgo, because they respect the Virgo's methodical nature. They'll also like encouraging their Virgo to relax and take life easy. Money will form a link between a Taurean and a Capricorn, with plenty of serious discussions on how to make it and what to do with it once they've got it. There will also be a strong sexual rapport, and the Taurean will encourage the more sensual side of the Capricorn.

The relationship between a Taurean and members of the Water element is also very good. A Taurean and a Cancerian will revel in one another's company and will probably be so happy at home that they'll rarely stir from their armchairs. They both have a strong need for emotional security and will stick together through thick and thin. There's plenty of passion when a Taurean pairs up with a Scorpio, although the faithful Taurean could become fed up with the Scorpio's jealous nature. They simply won't understand what they're being accused of, and their loyal nature will be offended by the very thought that they could be a two-timer. A Taurean will be delighted by a delicate Piscean, and will want to take care of such a vulnerable and sensitive creature.

Things become rather more complicated when a Taurean pairs up with an Arien, Leo or Sagittarian, all of whom are Fire signs. They have very little in common – Taureans like to take things slowly while Fire signs want to make things happen *now*. It's particularly difficult between a Taurean and an Arien – the careful Taurean will feel harried and rushed by the impetuous Arien. It's a little better when a Taurean gets together with a Leo, because they share a deep appreciation of the good things in life, although the Taurean will be horrified by the Leo's ability to spend money. Making joint decisions could be difficult, however, because they'll both stand their ground and refuse to budge. A Taurean and a Sagittarian simply don't understand each other – they're on such different wavelengths. Any Taurean displays of possessiveness will make the independent Sagittarian want to run a mile.

Taureans are equally mystified by the Air signs – Gemini, Libra and Aquarius. What they see as the flightiness of Gemini drives them barmy – why can't the Gemini settle down and do one thing at a time? The Taurean will probably feel quite exhausted by the Gemini's many interests and bubbly character. Taurus and Libra are a surprisingly good pairing, because they share a need for beauty, luxury and love. This could end up costing the penny-wise Taurean quite a packet, but they'll have a deliciously romantic time along the way. Taurus and Aquarius are chalk and cheese, and neither one is prepared to meet the other one halfway. The Taurean need to keep tabs on their loved one's every movement will irritate the freedom-loving Aquarian, and there will be plenty of rows as a result.

Compatibility in Love and Sex at a glance

F M	♈	♉	♊	♋	♌	♍	♎	♏	♐	♑	♒	♓
♈	8	5	9	7	9	4	7	8	9	7	7	3
♉	6	8	4	10	7	8	8	7	3	8	2	8
♊	8	2	7	3	8	7	9	4	9	4	9	4
♋	5	10	4	8	6	5	6	8	2	9	2	8
♌	9	8	9	7	7	4	9	6	8	7	9	6
♍	4	8	6	4	4	7	6	7	7	9	4	4
♎	7	8	10	7	8	5	9	6	9	6	10	6
♏	7	9	4	7	6	6	7	10	5	6	5	7
♐	9	4	10	4	9	7	8	4	9	6	9	5
♑	7	8	4	9	6	8	6	4	4	8	4	5
♒	8	6	9	4	9	4	9	6	8	7	8	2
♓	7	6	7	9	6	7	6	9	7	5	4	9

1 = the pits
10 = the peaks

Key

♈ – Aries
♉ – Taurus
♊ – Gemini
♋ – Cancer
♌ – Leo
♍ – Virgo

♎ – Libra
♏ – Scorpio
♐ – Sagittarius
♑ – Capricorn
♒ – Aquarius
♓ – Pisces

Compatibility in Friendship at a glance

F M	♈	♉	♊	♋	♌	♍	♎	♏	♐	♑	♒	♓
♈	8	5	10	5	9	3	7	8	9	6	8	5
♉	6	9	6	10	7	8	7	6	4	9	3	9
♊	9	3	9	4	9	8	10	5	10	5	10	6
♋	6	9	4	9	5	4	6	9	4	10	3	9
♌	10	7	9	6	9	4	8	6	9	6	9	7
♍	5	9	8	4	4	8	5	8	8	10	5	6
♎	8	9	10	8	8	6	9	5	9	6	10	7
♏	7	8	5	8	7	7	6	9	4	5	6	8
♐	9	5	10	4	10	8	8	4	10	7	9	6
♑	6	9	5	10	6	9	5	5	4	9	5	6
♒	9	6	10	5	9	5	9	7	9	5	9	3
♓	6	7	6	10	6	8	7	9	8	6	4	10

1 = the pits
10 = the peaks

Key

♈ – Aries
♉ – Taurus
♊ – Gemini
♋ – Cancer
♌ – Leo
♍ – Virgo

♎ – Libra
♏ – Scorpio
♐ – Sagittarius
♑ – Capricorn
♒ – Aquarius
♓ – Pisces

YOUR HOME AND FAMILY

What does your Sun sign say about the way you relate to your family? Is your home the most important thing in your life or is it simply somewhere you can get changed before going out on the town? Read on if you want to know more about your sign's attitude to home and family.

Gemini

If you are a typical Gemini, your home isn't the tidiest place in the street. Anything but, in fact! It is probably littered with newspapers and magazines that you haven't yet got around to reading, and piles of books that threaten to topple off the bookshelves. You make a point of buying the latest gadgets and machines if you can afford them, and can't resist the newest interactive technology. You prefer sunny, bright decorative schemes in styles that won't date. Your home may be filled with all the collections you enjoy amassing, from teapots to Russian icons. You like seeing your family but privately divide them into favourites and people you only see out of duty. Even so, you are always a lively participant at family gatherings and like catching up on all the news.

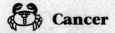 **Cancer**

Home is where your heart is. In fact, the two are practically inseparable in your eyes. You pine if you are away from home for too long and your heart always lifts when you re-enter your own little world. The kitchen is one of the most important rooms of the house for you, since you enjoy cooking and you adore eating. You will also want to spend money on a cosy sofa and a comfy bed. Photos of the family and treasured keepsakes decorate almost every available surface. When choosing furniture, you prefer items that are long-lasting and classic. If you can afford them, you will own lots of antiques. The family are never far away and you adore having them over to your place so you can feed them up.

 Leo

Your home is your castle. Even if your home is tiny, you lavish love and affection on it and are as proud of it as though it were an expensive mansion. Leos are very generous so you will want enough space to do some entertaining and, preferably, to have people to stay. If you can afford it, you enjoy treating yourself to the best that money can buy, from cushions to cookers. You are very family-minded and enjoy big gatherings of the clan. Children have a special place in your heart and you will make a huge fuss of the smallest members of the family. When decorating your home you will choose plenty of oranges and yellows, because these colours remind you of sunshine. You are good at creating an atmosphere, so may have a weakness for scented candles and oils. But only if they smell nice!

Virgo

Some people seem happy to live in a complete mess, but not you. Although Virgos aren't as tidy as is sometimes claimed, nevertheless you can't abide anything too grotty. Feng Shui might appeal to you because it emphasizes the need for clear space and lack of clutter, both of which are ideas that suit you well. You have a practical streak so don't want to fill your home with too many precious objects in case they get broken. You also prefer washable fabrics to those that have to be dry-cleaned. Virgos tend to be very nervy so it is important for you to have a restful bedroom in which you can sleep well. You enjoy being with your family but may limit your contact with them if they sometimes get on your nerves. You are easy to live with, provided everyone does their share of their chores and doesn't leave them up to you.

Libra

Pleasant surroundings are very important to you, and you will never be truly happy in anywhere that is mucky or ugly. That doesn't mean you have to live in a palace but you will make sure your home looks as good as possible. You like to furnish your home with unostentatious good taste. Even if you are rolling in money you don't want to look it. Antiques appeal to you, if you can afford them, because you like their traditional shapes and quality. And if you can't afford expensive antiques you may content yourself with going to your local junk shop and buying pieces of furniture that you can restore yourself at home. As for the family, you enjoy their company and want to let everyone have their turn in the conversational spotlight. However, you also enjoy your peace and quiet!

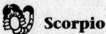

Scorpio

Privacy is essential for you. You are probably very selective about who you invite back to your home. It is as though they have to pass a test before they are allowed over the threshold, but after that they are welcome visitors. If you live with other people it is vital that you have a room of your own or somewhere that you can go to get away from everyone else, even if that simply means locking the bathroom door while you luxuriate in the bath. You are attracted to objects with a hint of mystery, and you enjoy decorating your home in a dramatic style, with lots of velvet, silk and low lighting. You adore your family and will defend them tooth and nail. When the chips are down, flesh and blood come first.

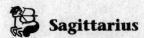

Sagittarius

It's highly likely that your home is decorated with trophies that you have brought back from your travels all over the world. Even if you have never ventured very far afield, there is still a cosmopolitan feeling to your home. You have an eclectic taste and enjoy collecting objects that catch your eye, trusting that everything will go together when you get them home. For instance, you might match Indian silks with Chinese plates and Dutch tiles. Books are an essential part of your life so your home is probably crammed to the rafters with them. You may even have written some of them yourself! Family mean a lot to you but you aren't as attached to them as some Sun signs. If you get on well with them they will become friends as well as family. If you don't really see eye to eye, you will keep your distance.

Capricorn

Tradition is very important to you, and this is usually obvious the moment anyone walks into your home. You love old objects and enjoy hunting around antique and junk shops so you can add to your treasures. Victoriana especially appeals to you. When looking for new furniture, you are attracted to items that will last – and last, and last. You hate the thought of spending money on anything that will soon date or fall apart. You are so canny that you may find you own objects that are worth much more than you paid for them, which is an unexpected bonus. Kith and kin come high up on your list of priorities and you set great store by family ties. Even if you disagree with someone's actions you will still support them in times of trouble.

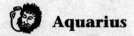

Aquarius

Unpredictable as always, your home could be a showcase of the latest contemporary styles or a homage to a bygone era. It all depends on how you are feeling, who you live with and how big your budget is. It's not that you don't care about your surroundings but you usually have your mind on more important topics than what colour curtains to have. There are neat rows of books, on a variety of subjects. You are fascinated by modern technology, so there will be an impressive array of electrical equipment. What most people don't expect is a traditional streak in you, making you faithfully remember the birthdays of everyone in the family. You especially enjoy talking to the younger members of the clan, encouraging them if necessary and letting them know that they can always come to you in a crisis.

 **Pisces**

You are one of the gentlest signs of the zodiac and your home reflects this. It is comfortable, relaxing and peaceful. It can feel like a refuge from a more jangled world, and if you have a garden it will be an oasis. You take great care over the way your home looks, with your collections of books, music and videos occupying prominent positions. Pisces is one of the most artistic signs so some of your paintings could be on the walls or your cushion covers may decorate the chairs. You enjoy taking photos too, and may embarrass the rest of the family when they see pictures of themselves at the age of two taking pride of place on the mantelpiece. Family is certainly very important to you and you like to keep in close contact with your nearest and dearest.

 Aries

Your sign is blessed with lots of energy, so you enjoy keeping busy around your home. If you move into somewhere that is more of a tip than ideal home, you will work your way steadily through all that DIY. It won't matter if you have never done it before – you will simply learn as you go along! What's more, you will cheerfully own up if you make mistakes, and turn them into funny stories that have everyone roaring with laughter. When decorating your home, you prefer items that are functional and simple. You can't bear frills or flounces! Your family mean a lot to you and you will always defend or support them when necessary. However, they may not see a lot of you because you have so many other interests in your life besides them.

 **Taurus**

Home is a very important place to you. Taurus is a highly practical sign and you can't help seeing your home as a cross between your own little universe and a good investment. In an ideal world, you will own your home as soon as possible, because it goes against the grain to pay rent instead of a mortgage. At heart, you are a real traditionalist so are much more interested in antiques and conventional furniture than anything very contemporary. Unless, of course, you know it will grow in value! Your home is full of natural materials, such as wood and stone, and plenty of plants. You need lots of space so family and friends can come to stay. It gives you great pleasure to curl up at home with your nearest and dearest gathered around you.